Simply Delicious

DIABETES COOKBOOK

Clockwise from upper left: Fresh Raspberry Fruit Spread (page 56), Parmesan Carrot Fries (page 139), Fiesta Lime Chicken Tacos (page 224), Strawberry Black Bean Barley Salad (page 170), Crispy Brown Rice and Quinoa Scotcheroos (page 290) Oatmeal–Whole Wheat–Blueberry Muffins (page 72)

BettyCrocker

Simply Delicious

DIABETES COOKBOOK

160+ NUTRITIOUS RECIPES FOR FOODS YOU LOVE

MARINER BOOKS

An Imprint of HarperCollins*Publishers*

Boston   New York

GENERAL MILLS

Chief Digital and Technology Officer:
Jaime Montemayor

Director, D&T, Enterprise Digital
Capabilities: Kelly Olin

Executive Editor: Cathy Swanson
Wheaton

Recipe Development and Testing:
Betty Crocker Kitchens

Photography: General Mills
Photography and Tony Kubat
Photography

Inspiring America to Cook at Home™

MARINER BOOKS
An Imprint of HarperCollins*Publishers*

Editorial Director: Karen Murgolo

Editor: Sarah Kwak

Senior Managing Editor:
Marina Padakis Lowry

Senior Editor: Christina Stambaugh

Art Director and book design:
Tai Blanche

Lead Production Coordinator:
Kimberly Kiefer

**Find more great ideas at
BettyCrocker.com**

marinerbooks.com

Library of Congress Cataloging-in-Publication Data has been applied for.

ISBN 978-0-358-65907-5 (pbk)

ISBN 978-0-358-65864-1 (ebk)

Manufactured in Italy

RTL 10 9 8 7 6 5 4 3 2 1

Cover photos clockwise from top left: Whole Wheat–Oat Pancakes with Raspberry-Apple Compote (page 60), Parmesan Carrot Fries (page 139), Watermelon-Strawberry Agua Fresca (page 336), Chicken Shawarma Meatball Pitas (page 230)

Back cover photos from top to bottom: Beef-Veggie Burgers with Honey-Horseradish Sauce (page 247), Garlicky Greens (page 205)

The content and recipes in this book have been reviewed with Registered Dietitians and nutrition experts at the General Mills' Bell Institute of Health and Nutrition. Please consult with your healthcare team for specific dietary needs and plans.

This book presents, among other things, the research and ideas of its author. It is not intended to be a substitute for consultation with a professional healthcare practitioner. Consult with your healthcare practitioner before starting any diet or other medical regimen. The publisher and the author disclaim responsibility for any adverse effects resulting directly or indirectly from information contained in this book.

Dear Food Lovers,

If you equate the word "diabetes" with unsatisfying, boring food that leaves your stomach growling, let this book open your world to new possibilities! In the Betty Crocker Kitchens, our heads are bursting with thoughts about how to make simple, achievable, yummy recipes. For this book, we've put on our thinking caps and created delicious recipes you'll love that are also diabetes friendly! And the best part? Everyone can enjoy them, whether living with diabetes or not, since they are the kinds of foods that are popular today. When we shot the photography for this book, the phrases that kept coming up were "I'd eat that" and "I can't believe you can eat this—I'd make it for sure!" What could be better than cooking only one meal that everyone enjoys together?

Living with diabetes just got tastier with the terrific basic recipes inside that you can make once and eat twice. There are also delicious recipes to cover your entire day—from breakfast through dinner, snacking and even desserts and beverages. There are recipes for rushed mornings, busy nights, entertaining and any craving.

Look for FAST for recipes that can be prepped in 20 minutes or less. Watch also for the topical features with helpful tips for:

Meal prepping	Adding flavor without salt
Carbohydrate counting	Eating out
Smart snacking	Enjoying dessert

Grab a fork and dive in!

Contents

Dive into Healthy and Delicious

Eating is one of life's joys, and a diabetes-friendly meal plan can be delicious, joyful *and* healthful. Food is intertwined with our lives, from filling our family's bellies to being part of our social gatherings and family celebrations. A diabetes-friendly meal plan can be sustainable and even en-JOY-able when you have satisfying recipes and tips that give you tools for a healthy eating plan.

MAKING IT SIMPLE TO MAKE WISE FOOD CHOICES

Here are some tips that are great to help you eat healthfully throughout your day. Work with your diabetes healthcare team to customize them specifically for you:

- **PLAN MEALS & SNACKS** If you don't plan, you could find yourself eating whatever is available, which may not always be the best choice. Set yourself up for success before you're ravenous and grabbing what's in front of you or entering the grocery store hungry. Planning what food you want to eat at home and while at work or school will help you stick to your meal plan. Check out Meal Prepping (page 22) for terrific ways to get a jump on quick meals. Planning may at first seem tedious, but just wait . . . on one of those typical hustle-and-bustle weeknights when you'd be normally desperate for a quick dinner or one of those days when you're always fighting the late-afternoon "hangries," the planning you've taken the time to do will pay off—and you'll be so glad for it!

- **EAT A VARIETY OF FOODS** Vegetables, fruits and grains are packed with vitamins, minerals and fiber—and each type brings its own "nutritional personality" to the table. Since each type of food differs in nutrient content from others, eating a variety helps ensure you get what your body needs. It also helps to avoid food boredom, and enhances the pleasure of eating. You will create a feast for the eyes and tongue by choosing a variety of colors, textures and flavors in the foods you mix and match.

- **CHOOSE WHOLE GRAINS** When eating foods made with grains, choose whole-grain options most of the time (such as whole wheat bread or whole-grain rolls instead of white bread or rolls, and whole-grain corn tortillas rather than flour tortillas). When eating side dishes, strive for veggie-based or whole-grain options most of the time (quinoa rather than white rice, or chick pea pasta rather than regular pasta).

- **DON'T SKIP MEALS** There are lots of reasons you may be tempted to skip meals. And many times, doing so may mean you end up overeating at the next meal. Stick to your meal plan, and talk to your healthcare team about snacks that would be appropriate for those times when it's not possible to have a regular meal.

HELPFUL NUTRITION AND COOKING INFORMATION

Criteria Used to Calculate Nutrition Information:

- The first ingredient was used whenever a choice is given (such as "⅓ cup yogurt or sour cream").

- The first ingredient amount was used whenever a range is given (such as "3- to 3½-pound cut-up whole chicken").

- The first serving number was used whenever a range is given (such as "4 to 6 servings").

- "If desired" ingredients and recipe variations were not included in the nutrition calculations.

- Only the amount of a marinade or frying oil that is estimated to be absorbed by the food during preparation or cooking was calculated.

GLUTEN-FREE, VEGETARIAN AND VEGAN RECIPES

- Special versions of ingredients were specified if necessary to claim a recipe is gluten free, vegetarian or vegan (such as vegan peanut butter). If it's not necessary for you to have the recipe be gluten free, vegetarian or vegan, you don't need to use the gluten-free, organic, pure or vegan versions of ingredients.

COOKING GLUTEN FREE AND VEGAN? Always read labels to make sure *each* recipe ingredient is gluten free and vegan. Products and ingredient sources can change.

INGREDIENTS AND EQUIPMENT USED IN RECIPE TESTING

- Large eggs and 2% milk were used unless otherwise indicated.

- Fat-free, low-fat, low-sodium or lite/light products were used only when indicated.

- Nonstick cookware and bakeware was used only when specified; dark-colored, black and insulated bakeware was not used.

- When a "pan" is called for, a metal pan was used; a "baking dish" or "pie plate" means ovenproof glass was used.

- Mixing was done by hand; when an electric hand mixer was used, the mixer speed is specified.

> **Following a diabetes-friendly meal plan is an opportunity to prepare and eat the best possible foods.**

Flavor-Packed Basics

Who doesn't love a two-fer? This one recipe makes chicken and broth to use in recipes calling for cooked chicken and/or broth. You can make the broth after dinner with very little effort while you clean up the kitchen! Use shallow containers for the broth so it can cool quickly to avoid any food safety issues.

CARB CHOICES

0

Reduced-Sodium* Roasted Chicken and Broth

PREP TIME: 25 Minutes / **START TO FINISH:** 2 Hours 15 Minutes / *5 cups broth and 5 cups cooked chicken*

- 1 cut-up whole chicken (3½ to 4 lb)
- 2 medium carrots or parsnips, quartered
- 2 medium stalks celery, quartered
- 1 medium onion, quartered
- 6 cups cold water
- ½ teaspoon salt
- ½ teaspoon pepper
- 1 sprig fresh parsley

1 Heat oven to 400°F. In ungreased 15×10×1-inch pan, arrange chicken, carrots, celery, and onion. Roast about 1 hour or until juice of chicken is clear when thickest piece is cut to bone, instant-read meat thermometer reads 165°F and pan juices are deep golden brown.

2 Cool slightly. Remove chicken from bones, reserving bones, skin, pan juices and any browned bits from bottom of pan. On cutting board, cut chicken into ½-inch pieces. Place chicken in food storage container; cover and refrigerate.

3 In 4-quart saucepan, place water, salt, pepper, parsley, roasted vegetables, chicken bones, skin, pan juices and browned bits. Heat to boiling; skim foam. Reduce heat to low. Cover; simmer about 30 minutes to develop flavors.

4 Carefully remove bones and skin from broth with slotted spoon. Strain broth through fine-mesh strainer; discard vegetables and parsley. Skim fat from broth by pouring broth in batches into fat separator, or pour broth into medium heatproof bowl. Cover; refrigerate until fat rises to the top and solidifies, then skim fat.

Storing Chicken and Broth Use chicken and broth immediately, or place chicken and broth in separate food storage containers. Cover; refrigerate up to 4 days or freeze up to 3 months.

1 CUP BROTH AND ½ CUP CHICKEN Calories 130; Total Fat 7g (Saturated Fat 2g, Trans Fat 0g); Cholesterol 50mg; Sodium 300mg; Total Carbohydrate 0g (Dietary Fiber 0g); Protein 16g **CARBOHYDRATE CHOICES:** 0

½ CUP CHICKEN Calories 100; Total Fat 4g (Saturated Fat 1g, Trans Fat 0g); Cholesterol 50mg; Sodium 50mg; Total Carbohydrate 0g (Dietary Fiber 0g); Protein 16g **CARBOHYDRATE CHOICES:** 0

1 CUP BROTH Calories 25; Total Fat 2.5g (Saturated Fat 1g, Trans Fat 0g); Cholesterol 0mg; Sodium 250mg; Total Carbohydrate 0g (Dietary Fiber 0g); Protein 0g **CARBOHYDRATE CHOICES:** 0

*Reduced-Sodium Roasted Chicken and Broth contains 43 percent less sodium than the original recipe. Sodium content has been lowered from 530mg to 300mg per serving.

Slow-Cooker Chicken Bone Broth Prepare roasted chicken as directed—except use 2 chickens and do not roast vegetables with the chickens. Remove meat from cooked chicken, reserving skin and bones; cut up and store chicken as directed. In 5- to 6-quart slow cooker insert, place bones, skin, the water, 2 tablespoons cider vinegar, the salt and pepper, the quartered onion, and the celery and carrots (peeled if desired), cut into 3-inch chunks. Add 6 cloves garlic and 4 sprigs fresh thyme. Increase parsley to 4 sprigs; add with thyme. Cover; cook on Low heat setting 10 to 12 hours. With slotted spoon, remove bones and skin. Strain broth through fine-mesh strainer into shallow food storage container; discard vegetables and herb sprigs. Cover; refrigerate overnight. Skim fat and discard.

Stock or broth? Stocks are typically made with bones, whereas broths are made with meat, not bones. But this recipe could also be called a "bone broth." This is a terrific use for your holiday bird. You can use this broth in recipes calling for chicken broth.

CARB CHOICES

0

Use-It-Up Turkey Stock

PREP TIME: 20 Minutes / **START TO FINISH:** 16 Hours 30 Minutes / *About 10 cups broth*

- 1 turkey carcass (from a roasted 10- to 12-lb turkey)
- 4 quarts water
- 2 large onions, chopped (2 cups)
- 1 cup coarsely chopped carrots
- 1 cup coarsely chopped celery
- 10 sprigs fresh parsley
- 3 sprigs thyme
- 1 teaspoon whole peppercorns

1 CUP Calories 50; Total Fat 3g (Saturated Fat 1g, Trans Fat 0g); Cholesterol 0mg; Sodium 340mg; Total Carbohydrate 0g (Dietary Fiber 0g); Protein 5g **CARBOHYDRATE CHOICES:** 0

Betty's Kitchen Tip Rather than throwing them away, save your cleaned carrot peels, celery tops, onion scraps and stripped parsley and thyme stems in a resealable freezer plastic bag. Toss them in the freezer until stock-making day. Then throw them in the pot with your poultry bones to add flavor to the stock.

Betty's Kitchen Tip Store this broth in 1 or 2 cup amounts, so it's easy to thaw just the right amount for your recipe.

1 In 8-quart or larger Dutch oven or stockpot, place turkey carcass. Cover with water; heat to boiling over high heat. Skim foam from top; reduce heat to medium-low. Simmer uncovered 6 hours, occasionally pushing carcass under the liquid.

2 Stir in remaining ingredients. Cook uncovered 2 hours longer.

3 Remove from heat. Cool 30 minutes. Carefully remove bones and skin from broth with slotted spoon. Strain stock through fine-mesh strainer; discard solids. Use immediately, or cool and ladle stock into food storage containers. Cover; refrigerate at least 2 hours or overnight. Skim fat from top of stock; discard fat. Use refrigerated stock within 3 to 4 days or freeze up to 6 months.

Flavorful and fall-off-the-bone tender, serve this chicken whole, as you would a roasted chicken, or remove the meat from the bones and cut it up or shred it into bite-size pieces to use in other recipes.

CARB CHOICES

$1/2$

Rotisserie-Style Chicken

PREP TIME: 10 Minutes / **START TO FINISH:** 2 Hours 50 Minutes / *6 servings*

2 tablespoons packed brown sugar

2 teaspoons chili powder

1 teaspoon salt

1 whole chicken (3 to 4 lb)

1 Spray 5-quart oval slow cooker with cooking spray.

2 In small bowl, stir together brown sugar, chili powder and salt.

3 Pat chicken dry, both inside and outside, with paper towels. Rub chicken all over with brown sugar mixture.

4 Place chicken, breast side up, in slow cooker. Cover; cook on High heat setting 2½ to 3½ hours or until legs move easily when lifted or twisted and instant-read meat thermometer inserted in thickest part of thigh reads 165°F. Remove chicken from slow cooker; let stand 10 minutes before serving.

1 SERVING Calories 250; Total Fat 14g (Saturated Fat 4g, Trans Fat 0g); Cholesterol 85mg; Sodium 500mg; Total Carbohydrate 5g (Dietary Fiber 0g); Protein 27g **CARBOHYDRATE CHOICES:** ½

Betty's Kitchen Tip If you like a little kick to your chicken, add ½ teaspoon ground red pepper (cayenne) to the brown sugar mixture.

Perfect for a crowd or for planned-ahead meals, this hearty pulled chicken can be used right away or packed into freezer-safe food storage containers. The saucy chicken would also be delicious in a bowl or as filling for tacos, burritos or enchiladas.

CARB CHOICES 2

Spicy Ancho Chicken Sandwiches

PREP TIME: 30 Minutes / **START TO FINISH:** 4 Hours 30 Minutes / *16 sandwiches*

- 1 can (28 oz) fire-roasted crushed tomatoes, undrained
- ¼ cup packed brown sugar
- ¼ cup ground ancho chile
- 1½ teaspoons kosher (coarse) salt
- 1 teaspoon dried oregano leaves
- ½ teaspoon ground red pepper (cayenne)
- ¼ cup cider vinegar
- 4 cloves garlic, cut in half
- 1 medium onion, sliced (1 cup)
- 2½ lb boneless skinless chicken breasts
- 16 whole wheat burger buns
  Sliced green onions, if desired

1 Spray 4- to 5-quart slow cooker with cooking spray. In blender, place tomatoes, brown sugar, ground chile, salt, oregano, red pepper, vinegar and garlic. Cover; blend on high speed until smooth. Pour about 1 cup of the tomato mixture into slow cooker. Spread out onion in slow cooker; top with chicken. Pour remaining tomato mixture over chicken.

2 Cover; cook on Low heat setting 3½ to 4 hours or until juice of chicken is clear when center of thickest part is cut and instant-read meat thermometer reads 165°F.

3 Turn off slow cooker. Remove chicken from cooker; cool slightly. Into 2-quart saucepan, spoon tomato mixture, onion and any juices. Heat to boiling; reduce heat. Simmer uncovered about 10 minutes, stirring occasionally, or until slightly thickened.

4 Meanwhile, shred chicken with 2 forks; return to slow cooker. Stir all but 1 cup of the tomato mixture into chicken. Set remaining tomato mixture aside.

5 Measure 1 cup of the tomato mixture; toss with chicken. Serve immediately or turn slow cooker on Warm or Low heat setting to keep chicken mixture warm. To serve, spoon about ½ cup chicken mixture into each bun; sprinkle with green onions. Serve with reserved sauce for dipping.

1 SANDWICH Calories 240; Total Fat 4g (Saturated Fat 1g, Trans Fat 0g); Cholesterol 45mg; Sodium 550mg; Total Carbohydrate 31g (Dietary Fiber 2g); Protein 21g **CARBOHYDRATE CHOICES:** 2

Betty's Kitchen Tip Ancho chiles are dried poblano chiles. They have an earthy, slightly sweet flavor that is mild to pungent, but they are not hot. We added ground red pepper to heat up these sandwiches. Add a bit more ground red pepper if you like your chicken spicier!

Betty's Kitchen Tip If you are serving this for a crowd and plan to keep it warm for more than 30 minutes, add another ¼ cup or so of the reserved sauce to the cooker to prevent the chicken from burning. Check occasionally to see if more sauce is needed.

Make Ahead Prepare as directed—except omit heating tomato mixture in Step 3. Add 1 cup of tomato mixture to shredded chicken in Step 5, but do not turn on slow cooker. Place chicken in food storage containers or resealable food-storage plastic bags. Pour remaining tomato mixture into separate food storage container. Cover; refrigerate chicken and tomato mixture up to 4 days or freeze up to 2 months. Thaw chicken and tomato mixture in refrigerator overnight. To serve, in saucepan, heat chicken and tomato mixture to boiling; reduce heat. Simmer covered, stirring occasionally, until hot, before serving in buns.

CARB CHOICES 0

If you don't have fresh herbs on hand or aren't going to the store, dried herbs can be used instead; just reduce the amount to ¼ teaspoon of each dried herb.

Roasted Herbed Turkey Breast

PREP TIME: 15 Minutes / **START TO FINISH:** 1 Hour 30 Minutes / *12 servings*

- 1 tablespoon butter, melted
- ½ teaspoon chopped fresh thyme leaves
- ½ teaspoon chopped fresh sage leaves
- 1 bone-in skin-on turkey breast half (2½ to 3 lb), patted dry
- 1 teaspoon salt
- ¼ teaspoon pepper

1 Heat oven to 325°F.

2 In small bowl, stir butter, thyme and sage until well mixed. Brush all sides of turkey breast with herb butter. Sprinkle with salt and pepper. Place skin side up on rack in 13×9-inch pan.

3 Roast uncovered 1 hour 30 to 2 hours or until instant-read meat thermometer in center reads 165°F. Remove from oven. Cover loosely with foil; let stand 10 minutes before slicing.

1 SERVING Calories 130; Total Fat 6g (Saturated Fat 2g, Trans Fat 0g); Cholesterol 50mg; Sodium 250mg; Total Carbohydrate 0g (Dietary Fiber 0g); Protein 18g **CARBOHYDRATE CHOICES:** 0

Air-Fryer Herbed Turkey Breast Cut piece of cooking parchment paper that will fit inside air fryer basket; place in bottom of basket. Spray with cooking spray. Prepare turkey breast as directed in Step 2. Place skin side up in basket. Set to 325°F; cook 30 minutes. Using tongs, carefully turn breast over. Cook 27 to 32 minutes or until instant-read meat thermometer reads 165°F. Remove from basket; let stand 10 minutes before slicing.

Betty's Kitchen Tip Air fryer temperature control settings vary according to brand and model. If your air fryer does not have the exact temperature setting called for in the recipe, consult your manual for suggested temperature settings.

Betty's Kitchen Tip Our recipes do not call for preheating the air fryer. Just set the temperature and start. Never preheat with cooking parchment paper alone.

MEAL PREPPING

Having appropriate foods ready to grab when you're hungry can help you stay on track.

The easiest way to make good choices is to plan for them! It puts you in control of the ingredients you eat and of portion sizes, so that when hunger hits, you're ready with delicious food that not only looks appealing but also satisfies *and* fits with your eating plan.

Cook Once, Eat Twice (Two-fers)

The easiest way to prep for meals is not to plan much at all! Simply make a recipe for one meal that will make enough to have for another as well. Many of the recipes in this chapter are designed for just that. Putting the second meal together is a lot less daunting when you've already got part of it finished, and only have to heat it up and round it out.

Strategize Your Shopping and Cooking

Another important key to success is to shop when you aren't hungry, so you aren't tempted to purchase groceries you don't need. And don't cook when you're so hungry that you're eating before the meal, sabotaging your dietary goals.

Think about what meals you struggle with the most. Are you ravenous when you wake up, or do you have no time midday to put together your lunch? Having things prepped and ready to grab during your busy times of the day prevents these potential roadblocks from ever being an issue.

Grab and Go Breakfasts

Spiced Lentil Breakfast Bowls, page 91

Chocolate-Banana Overnight Oats, page 80

Freezer Breakfast Tortilla Stacks, page 103

FOODS BELOW FROM LEFT TO RIGHT:

1. Strawberry Black Bean Barley Salad (page 170), celery and spinach

2. Leaf lettuce salad with chick peas, hard-cooked egg and carrot sticks

3. Protein-added spaghetti, Freezer-Friendly Turkey Meatballs (page 25), Strawberry Barbecue Sauce (page 53), Cumin-Citrus Roasted Carrots (page 208)

4. Brown rice, Make-Ahead Mexican-Style Turkey Sausage (page 30), scrambled eggs, sautéed zucchini, tomatoes and onion

5. Roasted Herbed Turkey Breast (page 20), quinoa, sautéed red bell pepper and broccoli

Meatballs are so versatile—use them in bowls, served with eggs or pasta, or in sandwiches or even on pizza! Having them at the ready means meals are a snap to put together.

CARB CHOICES 1/2

Freezer-Friendly Turkey Meatballs

PREP TIME: 35 Minutes / **START TO FINISH:** 1 Hour 5 Minutes / *16 servings (3 meatballs each)*

- 6 slices whole wheat sandwich bread
- 1 medium onion, quartered
- 5 cloves garlic
- 2 packages (16 oz each) ground turkey (at least 93% lean)
- 2 eggs, beaten
- ⅔ cup fat-free (skim) milk
- 1 tablespoon Dijon mustard
- 1¼ teaspoons salt
- 1 teaspoon Worcestershire sauce

1 SERVING Calories 130; Total Fat 6g (Saturated Fat 1.5g, Trans Fat 0g); Cholesterol 65mg; Sodium 290mg; Total Carbohydrate 6g (Dietary Fiber 0g); Protein 13g **CARBOHYDRATE CHOICES:** ½

Betty's Kitchen Tip Use a 1½-inch-diameter cookie scoop to quickly measure the right amount of turkey mixture for each meatball.

To Freeze Meatballs Cool meatballs on pans 15 minutes. Place cooled meatballs on cooking parchment paper–lined cookie sheet; cover with plastic wrap and freeze until firm, at least 2 hours. Place frozen meatballs in resealable freezer plastic bags. Store in freezer and use within 6 months.

To Reheat Meatballs To reheat, place 12 meatballs (4 servings) in single layer on microwavable dish; cover with plastic wrap. Microwave on Medium (50%) until hot (instant-read meat thermometer reads 165°F), rotating meatballs halfway through cooking. For frozen meatballs, microwave 7 to 8 minutes; for refrigerated, microwave 2 minutes 30 seconds to 4 minutes 30 seconds.

1 Move 2 oven racks to upper and lower thirds of oven. Heat oven to 400°F. Line two 15×10×1-inch pans with cooking parchment paper or foil; spray with cooking spray.

2 Tear bread into large pieces. In food processor, place half the bread. Cover; process with 8 to 10 on-and-off pulses or until crumbs form. In large bowl, place bread crumbs. Repeat with remaining bread.

3 In food processor, place onion and garlic. Cover; process with 8 to 10 on-and-off pulses, scraping bowl once, until finely chopped. Add onion and remaining ingredients to bread mixture; mix gently just until blended. Shape into 1½-inch meatballs; place on pans ½ inch apart.

4 Bake 25 to 30 minutes, rotating pans between racks halfway through, until meatballs begin to brown and instant-read meat thermometer inserted in center of meatballs reads 165°F. Serve warm, refrigerate and use within 4 days or freeze for another use following directions at right.

Make this recipe for dinner, then use the remaining beef for Roast Beef with Parsnip-Potato Mash and Mushroom Gravy (page 244), and get a jump-start on a restaurant-worthy meal.

CARB CHOICES

1

Roast Beef and Vegetables

PREP TIME: 25 Minutes / **START TO FINISH:** 7 Hours 25 Minutes / *8 servings beef and 4 servings vegetables*

4 medium carrots, cut into fourths

3 small turnips, ends trimmed, quartered

2 medium red potatoes, quartered

1 small red onion, chopped (½ cup)

2½ teaspoons fresh thyme leaves

1 boneless beef chuck roast (2½ to 2¾ lb)

½ teaspoon salt

½ teaspoon pepper

Roast Beef Gravy (see page 28), if desired

1 Spray 5- to 6-quart slow cooker with cooking spray. Place half of the carrots, turnips, potatoes and onion and 1 teaspoon of the thyme in slow cooker.

2 Sprinkle beef with salt and pepper. Heat 12-inch nonstick skillet over medium-high heat. Cook beef in skillet, 1 to 2 minutes on each side, or until browned. Place beef on top of vegetables in slow cooker; top with remaining vegetables and 1 teaspoon of the remaining thyme.

3 Cover; cook on Low heat setting 7 to 8 hours or until beef is tender. Remove beef from slow cooker. Cut beef in half; store one portion for another meal (see sidenote at right). Place remaining portion on serving platter. Using slotted spoon, transfer vegetables to serving platter. Sprinkle beef and vegetables with remaining ½ teaspoon thyme.

4 If preparing the Roast Beef Gravy, cover beef and vegetables with foil to keep warm and reserve 1¼ cups drippings from slow cooker to use for making the gravy. Prepare Roast Beef Gravy; serve with beef and vegetables.

1 SERVING (BEEF AND VEGETABLES) Calories 300; Total Fat 14g (Saturated Fat 5g, Trans Fat 0.5g); Cholesterol 70mg; Sodium 290mg; Total Carbohydrate 20g (Dietary Fiber 4g); Protein 26g **CARBOHYDRATE CHOICES:** 1

1 SERVING (BEEF ONLY) Calories 210; Total Fat 13g (Saturated Fat 5g, Trans Fat 0.5g); Cholesterol 70mg; Sodium 200mg; Total Carbohydrate 0g (Dietary Fiber 0g); Protein 23g **CARBOHYDRATE CHOICES:** 0

Betty's Kitchen Tip How tender do you like your beef? You can cook the beef just until a fork can be poked into the meat with little resistance—it will be great for slicing. If you like it very tender, cook it until the fork goes into the beef very easily (like softened butter) and it will just fall apart when served.

Storing Remaining Beef **To refrigerate,** place beef in food storage container. Cover; refrigerate up to 3 days. **To freeze,** wrap beef in foil; label and freeze up to 3 months. Before reheating, thaw frozen beef 12 to 24 hours in refrigerator. **To reheat in oven,** unwrap beef, slice and place slices in single layer on large clean sheet of foil; fold foil to enclose beef and place on cookie sheet. Bake at 350°F for 30 to 35 minutes or until hot (instant-read meat thermometer reads 165°F). **To reheat in microwave,** unwrap beef, slice and place slices in single layer on microwavable dish; cover with plastic wrap. Microwave on Medium (50%) about 4 minutes or until hot (instant-read meat thermometer reads 165°F).

This recipe is perfect for using up drippings from roasted meat, but if you don't have leftover drippings, you can use the Butter Gravy variation.

CARB CHOICES

0

Roast Beef Gravy

PREP TIME: 15 Minutes / **START TO FINISH:** 15 Minutes / *16 servings (1 tablespoon each)*

Drippings from Roast Beef and Vegetables (page 26)

2 tablespoons all-purpose flour

⅛ teaspoon coarse ground black pepper

1 teaspoon low-sodium soy sauce

1 Pour drippings into fat separator. Reserve 2 tablespoons fat; discard remaining fat. Or pour drippings into 2-cup measure, cover and refrigerate until fat rises to the top and solidifies. Reserve 1 cup cooking liquid (discard remaining liquid). If there is not enough cooking liquid, add water to make 1 cup.

2 In 1-quart saucepan, heat reserved fat over medium heat until melted. Stir in flour and pepper; cook 1 minute, stirring frequently.

3 Gradually stir in reserved cooking liquid with whisk until smooth. Stir in soy sauce. Heat to boiling. Reduce heat; cook, uncovered, 1 to 3 minutes, stirring occasionally, or until gravy is thickened.

1 SERVING Calories 110; Total Fat 11g (Saturated Fat 4.5g, Trans Fat 0.5g); Cholesterol 15mg; Sodium 15mg; Total Carbohydrate 0g (Dietary Fiber 0g); Protein 2g **CARBOHYDRATE CHOICES:** 0

Butter Gravy Prepare as directed above except substitute 2 tablespoons butter and 1 cup reduced-sodium beef or chicken broth for the fat and cooking liquid.

Mild vegetables are preferred for a well-balanced, neutral flavor. Broccoli, rutabaga, red cabbage or other strong-flavored vegetables would overpower the broth, and may give it a muddy, objectionable color.

CARB CHOICES

0

Reduced-Sodium* Vegetable Broth

PREP TIME: 20 Minutes / **START TO FINISH:** 1 Hour 50 Minutes / *8 cups broth*

- 8 cups cold water
- 6 cups coarsely chopped mild vegetables (such as bell peppers, carrots, celery, leeks, mushrooms**, potatoes, spinach and/or zucchini)
- 1 small onion, coarsely chopped (½ cup)
- 4 cloves garlic, finely chopped

- ½ cup lightly-packed fresh parsley sprigs
- 2 tablespoons chopped fresh or 2 teaspoons dried basil leaves
- 2 tablespoons chopped fresh or 2 teaspoons dried thyme leaves
- ½ teaspoon salt
- ¼ teaspoon cracked black pepper
- 2 dried bay leaves

1 In 4-quart saucepan, mix all ingredients. Heat to boiling; reduce heat. Cover; simmer 1 hour, stirring occasionally.

2 Cool 30 minutes. Strain broth through fine-mesh strainer; discard solids. Use immediately or cool and ladle into food storage containers. Cover; refrigerate up to 4 days or freeze up to 6 months. Stir before using.

1 CUP Calories 15; Total Fat 0g (Saturated Fat 0g, Trans Fat 0g); Cholesterol 0mg; Sodium 160mg; Total Carbohydrate 3g (Dietary Fiber 1g); Protein 0g **CARBOHYDRATE CHOICES:** 0

Betty's Kitchen Tip This is a great recipe to make if you have veggies in your fridge that aren't getting used up quick enough, so that they don't go to waste.

*Reduced-sodium vegetable broth contains 75 percent less sodium than store-bought vegetable broth. Sodium content has been lowered from 650mg to 160mg per serving.

**Some mushrooms have woody stems that cannot be eaten, but they can be used to flavor the broth.

Here's a sneaky way to keep the lid on sodium. Use this meat as the filling for tacos, burritos or enchiladas. By the time you add all the veggie toppings to your Mexican-inspired dishes, you'll have a party of flavor and will never miss the sodium in your meat!

CARB CHOICES

0

Make-Ahead Mexican-Style Ground Beef

PREP TIME: 15 Minutes / **START TO FINISH:** 1 Hour 20 Minutes / *8 cups*

3 lb lean ground beef (at least 80%)

¾ cup water

1 batch Salt-Free Taco Seasoning Mix (page 40)

1 In 5-quart Dutch oven, cook beef over medium-high heat about 10 minutes, stirring occasionally, or until thoroughly cooked; drain.

2 Reduce heat to medium. Stir in water and seasoning mix. Cook 3 to 5 minutes, stirring frequently, or until liquid is absorbed and flavors are blended. Cool 5 minutes.

3 Line 15×10×1-inch pan with foil. Spread beef in pan. Freeze about 1 hour, stirring once, until firm.

4 Place 2 cups of the beef mixture in each freezer-safe food storage container or resealable freezer plastic bag; seal tightly. Freeze up to 3 months.

½ CUP Calories 160; Total Fat 10g (Saturated Fat 3.5g, Trans Fat 0g); Cholesterol 50mg; Sodium 70mg; Total Carbohydrate 2g (Dietary Fiber 0g); Protein 15g **CARBOHYDRATE CHOICES:** 0

Make-Ahead Mexican-Style Ground Turkey Substitute ground turkey (at least 93% lean) for ground beef.

Make-Ahead Mexican-Style Turkey Sausage Substitute bulk turkey sausage for ground beef.

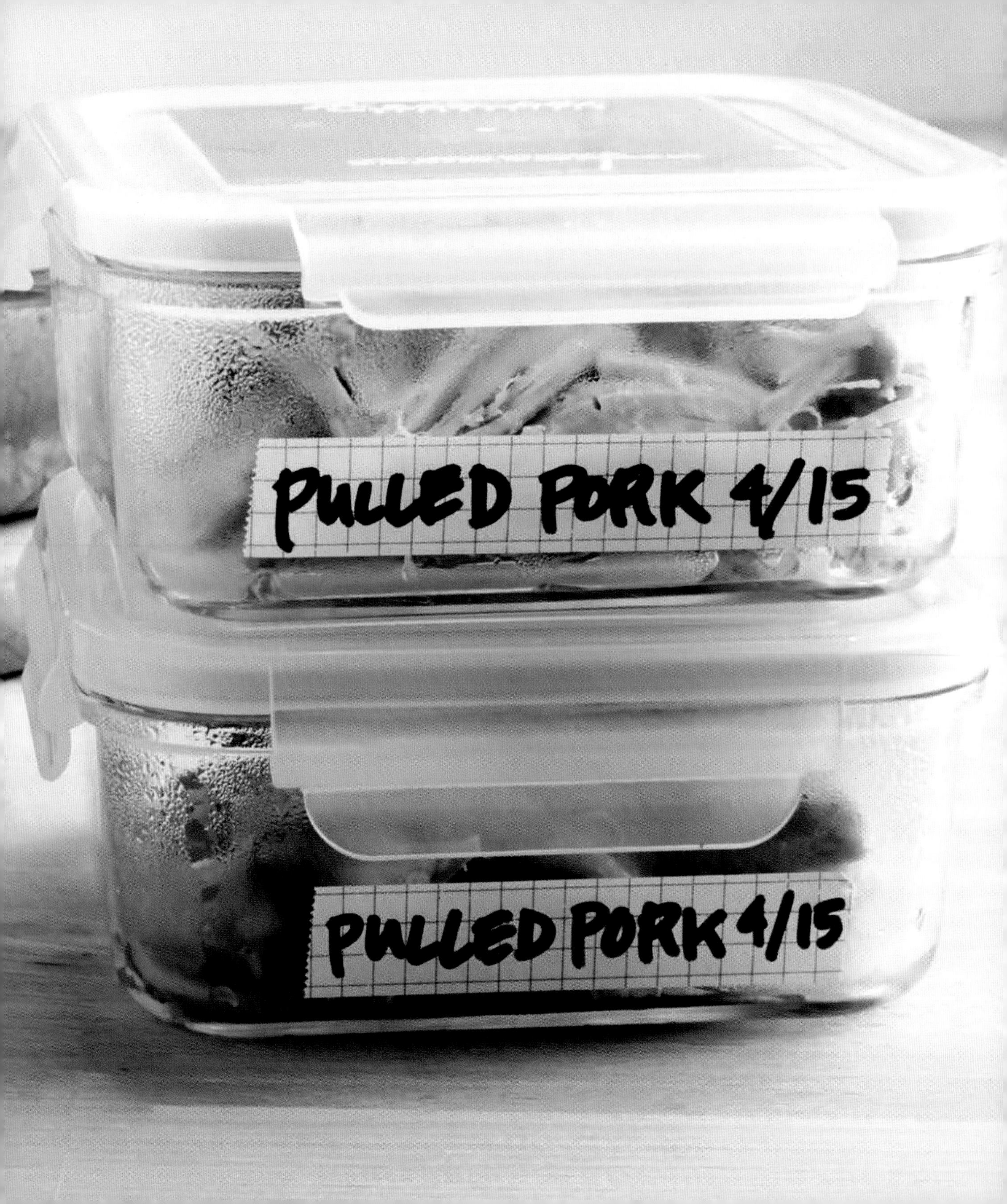
PULLED PORK 4/15
PULLED PORK 4/15

We recommended freezing the pork in 2-cup portions for an average family size of four, but make it work for you by packaging in whatever size portion you need to feed your family for one meal.

CARB CHOICES

0

Make-Ahead Oven-Roasted Pulled Pork

PREP TIME: 15 Minutes / **START TO FINISH:** 8 Hours 15 Minutes / *10 cups*

1 boneless pork shoulder roast (5 lb)

20 cloves garlic, peeled

3 tablespoons olive oil

1½ teaspoons salt

2 teaspoons pepper

1 Heat oven to 325°F. In 13×9-inch (3-quart) glass baking dish, place pork, fat side up. With sharp knife, cut (20) 1-inch slits in fat; tuck 1 clove garlic into each slit. Rub pork with oil. Sprinkle with salt and pepper; rub into meat.

2 Cover tightly with foil. Roast 5 hours 30 minutes to 6 hours 30 minutes or until instant-read meat thermometer inserted in center of roast reads 190°F. Let stand until cool enough to handle, about 30 minutes.

3 Shred meat with 2 forks; discard garlic. Toss shredded pork in some of the pan juices (if any) to coat. Use immediately or divide into 2-cup portions; place in freezer-safe food storage containers or resealable freezer plastic bags. Seal tightly; refrigerate until completely cooled, at least 1 hour. Freeze up to 3 months.

½ **CUP** Calories 230; Total Fat 15g (Saturated Fat 5g, Trans Fat 0g); Cholesterol 70mg; Sodium 220mg; Total Carbohydrate 1g (Dietary Fiber 0g); Protein 23g **CARBOHYDRATE CHOICES:** 0

You can make this recipe for dinner and have enough cooked barley on hand for two other meals, depending on how you use it.

Make-Ahead Cilantro-Lime Barley

PREP TIME: 10 Minutes / **START TO FINISH:** 55 Minutes / *15 servings (⅓ cup each)*

1 lime
3½ cups reduced-sodium chicken broth (for homemade broth, see page 12)
1 cup light beer or water
1½ cups uncooked hulled barley
3 cloves garlic, finely chopped

1 tablespoon chopped fresh cilantro

ADDITIONAL STIR-INS FOR REMAINING BARLEY

2 tablespoons chopped fresh cilantro
2 teaspoons lime zest

1 Zest lime to equal 1 teaspoon lime zest; set aside. Juice lime to equal 2 tablespoons.

2 In 3-quart saucepan, heat broth and beer over high heat until boiling. Add barley, lime juice and garlic; stir. Reduce heat to low. Cover; simmer 45 to 50 minutes or until barley is tender and almost all liquid is absorbed. Measure 1⅔ cups barley into serving bowl; stir in reserved lime zest and 1 tablespoon chopped cilantro. Serve warm.

3 Line two 15×10×1-inch pans with cooking parchment paper. Spread remaining barley on pans in single layer; cool completely, about 10 minutes. Spoon barley into two 2-cup microwavable freezer-safe food storage containers. Refrigerate up to 4 days or freeze up to 6 months.

4 If frozen, thaw barley in refrigerator overnight. For each container, remove lid from container and cover loosely with plastic wrap. Microwave on High 2 to 2½ minutes or until hot. Stir 1 tablespoon of the additional cilantro and 1 teaspoon of the lime zest into rice and serve.

1 SERVING Calories 90; Total Fat 0.5g (Saturated Fat 0g, Trans Fat 0g); Cholesterol 0mg; Sodium 20mg; Total Carbohydrate 17g (Dietary Fiber 3g); Protein 3g **CARBOHYDRATE CHOICES:** 1

Roasting vegetables is a great way to add flavor and texture to a meal. It softens their interiors to just the right tender texture, adds a bit of crispiness to the edges, and brings out richer flavor than you'd ever get from steamed or raw veggies. Prepare these for dinner, then save the remaining veggies for other meals during the week. If you store the veggies by type, you can enjoy different veggies at different meals!

CARB CHOICES 1/2

Roasted Sweet Potatoes and Vegetables

PREP TIME: 20 Minutes / **START TO FINISH:** 50 Minutes / *12 servings (about ½ cup each)*

⅓ cup sliced green onions (about 5 medium)

2 tablespoons olive oil

½ teaspoon salt

¼ teaspoon pepper

3 cups diced (¾-inch) peeled orange-fleshed sweet potatoes

1 cup diced (¾-inch) red bell pepper (about 1 large)

3 cups broccoli florets (about 7 oz)

1 cup frozen peas

2 tablespoons chopped fresh cilantro

1 Heat oven to 425°F. Line 18×13-inch half-sheet pan with cooking parchment paper; spray with cooking spray. Reserve 1 tablespoon onion.

2 In large bowl, mix 1 tablespoon of the olive oil, ¼ teaspoon of the salt and ⅛ teaspoon of the pepper. Add sweet potatoes and red bell pepper; toss to coat. Transfer vegetables to pan and spread in single layer; set aside bowl. Roast 20 minutes; stir.

3 In same bowl, place remaining 1 tablespoon olive oil, ¼ teaspoon salt and ⅛ teaspoon pepper. Add broccoli, peas and remaining onion; toss to coat. Stir into vegetable mixture in pan. Roast 10 minutes or until peas are heated through and sweet potatoes are tender. Top with reserved onion and cilantro.

1 SERVING Calories 70; Total Fat 2.5g (Saturated Fat 0g, Trans Fat 0g); Cholesterol 0mg; Sodium 130mg; Total Carbohydrate 10g (Dietary Fiber 2g); Protein 1g **CARBOHYDRATE CHOICES:** ½

Betty's Kitchen Tip Use a pancake turner to turn the veggies, as they can stick to the pan when browning.

Betty's Kitchen Tip To use veggies for other meals, omit cilantro. Cool in pan to room temperature. Spoon into food storage containers. Cover; refrigerate up to 4 days. To reheat, just before serving, uncover and microwave on High until hot. Or serve at room temperature. Sprinkle with reserved onion and cilantro just before serving.

This sauce is great to have on hand for quick meals. It is lower in sodium and sugar* than many of the most popular brands. Ladle the cooked sauce into freezer-safe food storage containers, and keep in your freezer up to a month. Just thaw in the refrigerator or microwave, then use in your favorite recipe. For even less sodium, you can use no-salt-added crushed tomatoes and add ½ teaspoon dried basil leaves.

CARB CHOICES

½

Classic Marinara Sauce

PREP TIME: 10 Minutes / **START TO FINISH:** 25 Minutes / *6 servings* (*½ cup each*)

1 tablespoon olive or vegetable oil

1 small onion, chopped (½ cup)

¼ cup finely chopped carrot

2 cloves garlic, finely chopped

1 can (28 oz) organic crushed tomatoes with basil, undrained

1 tablespoon chopped fresh Italian (flat-leaf) parsley

½ teaspoon chopped fresh or ¼ teaspoon dried oregano leaves

¼ teaspoon coarse (kosher or sea) salt

¼ teaspoon pepper

1 In 3-quart saucepan, heat oil over medium heat. Add onion, carrot and garlic; cook about 5 minutes, stirring occasionally, or until tender. Stir in remaining ingredients.

2 Heat to boiling; reduce heat. Cover; simmer 15 minutes.

3 Serve over cooked pasta as desired.

1 SERVING Calories 70; Total Fat 2.5g (Saturated Fat 0g, Trans Fat 0g); Cholesterol 0mg; Sodium 320mg; Total Carbohydrate 10g (Dietary Fiber 1g); Protein 1g **CARBOHYDRATE CHOICES:** ½

*Classic Marinara Sauce contains 32 percent less sodium and 50 percent less sugar than regular, store-bought marinara.

Use this homemade taco seasoning in any recipe calling for the store-bought version. The beauty of this mix is that you can control the salt in your food by adding salt to taste to the finished dish. A quarter cup of this mix is equal to a 1-ounce package of purchased taco seasoning mix.

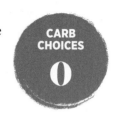

CARB CHOICES

0

Salt-Free Taco Seasoning Mix

PREP TIME: 5 Minutes / **START TO FINISH:** 5 Minutes / *About ½ cup*

2 tablespoons chili powder

1 tablespoon onion powder

5 teaspoons ground cumin

5 teaspoons paprika

2½ teaspoons garlic powder

⅛ to ¼ teaspoon ground red pepper (cayenne)

In small container with tight-fitting lid, mix all ingredients until well blended; cover. Store in cool, dry place up to 6 months. Stir or shake well before using.

1 TEASPOON Calories 10; Total Fat 0g (Saturated Fat 0g, Trans Fat 0g); Cholesterol 0mg; Sodium 10mg; Total Carbohydrate 1g (Dietary Fiber 0g); Protein 0g **CARBOHYDRATE CHOICES:** 0

Smoky Salt-Free Taco Seasoning Mix

Substitute 2 teaspoons smoked paprika for 2 teaspoons of the regular paprika.

This amazing classic sauce is full of flavor and so versatile! Try it with breakfast eggs, as a sauce for plain chicken, fish or meat, or stir it into cooked rice or cooked grains. It's also a terrific choice as a salad dressing or dip.

CARB CHOICES

0

Salsa

PREP TIME: 15 Minutes / **START TO FINISH:** 1 Hour 15 Minutes / *3½ cups*

- 3 large tomatoes, seeded, finely chopped (3 cups)
- ½ finely chopped green bell pepper
- 8 medium green onions, sliced (½ cup)
- 3 cloves garlic, finely chopped

- 2 tablespoons chopped fresh cilantro
- 2 to 3 tablespoons lime juice
- 1 tablespoon finely chopped seeded jalapeño chile
- ½ teaspoon salt

In medium glass or plastic bowl, mix all ingredients. Cover; refrigerate at least 1 hour to blend flavors. Store covered in refrigerator up to 1 week.

¼ **CUP** Calories 15; Total Fat 0g (Saturated Fat 0g, Trans Fat 0g); Cholesterol 0mg; Sodium 90mg; Total Carbohydrate 3g (Dietary Fiber 0g); Protein 0g **CARBOHYDRATE CHOICES:** 0

Black Bean Salsa Stir in 1 can (15 oz) black beans, rinsed and drained. Makes about 5 cups.

Mango-Pepper Salsa Omit tomatoes, substitute 1 red bell pepper for the green bell pepper, reduce green onions to 1 tablespoon. Add 1 cup peeled, pitted and diced mango. Makes about 1½ cups.

Think of it as salsa's chunky cousin! While salsa tends to be smoother and used as a sauce, pico de gallo is chunkier and used as a condiment. Or use it in salads or baked recipes that call for tomatoes and onions to get a jump on your meal prep.

CARB CHOICES

0

Pico de Gallo

PREP TIME: 15 Minutes / **START TO FINISH:** 15 Minutes / *10 servings (¼ cup each)*

2 large ripe tomatoes, seeded and chopped

¼ cup chopped red onion

¼ cup chopped green bell pepper

3 tablespoons finely chopped seeded jalapeño chile (1 large)

2 tablespoons chopped fresh cilantro leaves

2 tablespoons fresh lime juice

¼ teaspoon sea salt

In medium bowl, mix all ingredients.

1 SERVING Calories 10; Total Fat 0g (Saturated Fat 0g, Trans Fat 0g); Cholesterol 0mg; Sodium 60mg; Total Carbohydrate 2g (Dietary Fiber 0g); Protein 0g **CARBOHYDRATE CHOICES:** 0

Betty's Kitchen Tip Make this several hours in advance and refrigerate covered, so it will have time to blend flavors and be even more delicious.

Make It Your Own Change it up by using orange or yellow bell peppers in place of green bell peppers.

Tomatillos look like small green (unripe) tomatoes covered with papery husks; remove the husks and rinse off any sticky residue before chopping.

Tomatillo Salsa

PREP TIME: 30 Minutes / **START TO FINISH:** 30 Minutes / *32 servings (2 tablespoons each)*

1½ lb fresh tomatillos, husks removed, rinsed

2 to 3 serrano chiles, seeded

2 large cloves garlic, peeled

1 medium white onion, coarsely chopped (1 cup)

¼ cup coarsely chopped fresh cilantro

¾ cup gluten-free reduced-sodium chicken broth (for homemade broth, see page 12)

½ teaspoon salt

½ teaspoon gluten-free chicken bouillon granules

2 tablespoons canola oil

1 In 3-quart saucepan, place tomatillos; cover with cold water. Cook over medium heat 10 to 15 minutes or until tender. Drain; discard water.

2 In blender, mix tomatillos and remaining ingredients except oil. Cover; blend until desired consistency.

3 In 2-quart saucepan, heat oil over medium heat. Add tomatillo mixture. Cook 10 to 15 minutes, stirring constantly, or until mixture is thoroughly heated and darker in color. Serve warm or cool to room temperature; spoon into food storage container. Cover and refrigerate up to 1 week and serve cold.

1 SERVING Calories 20; Total Fat 1g (Saturated Fat 0g, Trans Fat 0g); Cholesterol 0mg; Sodium 60mg; Total Carbohydrate 2g (Dietary Fiber 0g); Protein 0g **CARBOHYDRATE CHOICES:** 0

Tomatillo
Salsa

Traditionally heavy on olive oil, this skinny version of pesto is delicious on chicken and cooked vegetables, stirred into brown rice, dolloped on top of burgers . . . the possibilities are endless. And you won't miss the extra oil! You can also substitute parsley or cilantro for the basil for a tasty twist.

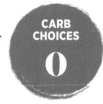

CARB CHOICES

0

Skinny Pesto

PREP TIME: 10 Minutes / **START TO FINISH:** 10 Minutes / *16 servings (1 tablespoon each)*

- 2 cups fresh firmly packed basil leaves (about 3 oz)
- ½ cup grated Parmesan cheese
- ½ cup gluten-free reduced-sodium chicken broth (for homemade broth, see page 12)
- ¼ cup pine nuts or walnuts
- 2 tablespoons olive oil
- ¼ teaspoon pepper
- 4 cloves garlic, coarsely chopped

1 In food processor or blender, place all ingredients. Cover; process on high speed 2 to 3 minutes, stopping occasionally to scrape down sides with rubber spatula, until smooth.

2 Use immediately or cover tightly and refrigerate no longer than 24 hours (color of pesto will darken as it stands) or freeze up to 1 month.

1 SERVING Calories 45; Total Fat 4g (Saturated Fat 1g, Trans Fat 0g); Cholesterol 0mg; Sodium 60mg; Total Carbohydrate 0g (Dietary Fiber 0g); Protein 2g **CARBOHYDRATE CHOICES:** 0

Let's just say it . . . yum! We've used this sauce for our Thai-Style Noodles and Veggies (page 273), but you can use it for grilled chicken, fish or pasta dishes. Don't miss the Peanut Coriander Dressing variation. We've used it on the Thai-Style Chopped Salad (page 162), but its unique ingredient combination would make a nice change of pace on any green salad as well.

CARB CHOICES

1/2

Thai Peanut-Coconut Sauce

PREP TIME: 10 Minutes / **START TO FINISH:** 10 Minutes / *10 servings (2 tablespoons each)*

½ cup reduced-fat creamy peanut butter

¼ cup unsweetened coconut milk (from 13.66-oz can; not cream of coconut)

¼ cup rice vinegar

3 tablespoons gluten-free reduced-sodium soy sauce

1 tablespoon finely chopped gingerroot

1 tablespoon chopped Thai basil or regular basil leaves

1½ teaspoons lime zest

1 teaspoon toasted sesame oil

½ teaspoon Asian chili garlic sauce

In small bowl, beat all ingredients with whisk until blended. Store tightly covered in refrigerator up to 3 days. Stir well before using.

1 SERVING SAUCE Calories 90; Total Fat 5g (Saturated Fat 1g, Trans Fat 0g); Cholesterol 0mg; Sodium 250mg; Total Carbohydrate 6g (Dietary Fiber 1g); Protein 4g **CARBOHYDRATE CHOICES:** ½

Peanut Coriander Dressing In small bowl, place ⅓ cup Thai Peanut Coconut Sauce. Stir in 3 tablespoons unsweetened coconut milk and ½ teaspoon ground coriander.

2 TEASPOONS DRESSING Calories 80; Total Fat 6g (Saturated Fat 2.5g, Trans Fat 0g); Cholesterol 0mg; Sodium 170mg; Total Carbohydrate 4g (Dietary Fiber 0g); Protein 3g **CARBOHYDRATE CHOICES:** 0

Marinades are a great way to infuse flavor into poultry, meat or veggies so they burst with great taste. Mark this page as a go-to whenever you're getting bored with plain meat or vegetables.

CARB CHOICES

0

Mediterranean Herb Marinade

PREP TIME: 15 Minutes / **START TO FINISH:** 15 Minutes / *6 servings (1 tablespoon each)*

¼ cup olive oil

1 teaspoon lemon zest

¼ cup fresh lemon juice

3 tablespoons chopped fresh oregano leaves

2 tablespoons chopped fresh rosemary leaves

3 cloves garlic, finely chopped

½ teaspoon salt

½ teaspoon pepper

1 In shallow glass or plastic bowl or resealable food-storage plastic bag, mix all ingredients.

2 Add 1 to 2 pounds boneless or 2 to 3 pounds bone-in chicken, turkey, beef or pork; 1 to 2 pounds fish or seafood; about 14 ounces cubed tofu; or up to 4 cups cut-up fresh vegetables. Turn to coat food with marinade. Cover dish or seal bag. Let tofu marinate at room temperature, or fish, seafood or vegetables in the refrigerator, no longer than 30 minutes; refrigerate beef, pork or poultry at least 1 hour but no longer than 24 hours. Turn food occasionally.

3 Remove poultry, meat, fish or seafood, tofu or vegetables from marinade. Cook as desired, brushing occasionally with marinade while cooking. Discard remaining marinade.

1 SERVING Calories 90; Total Fat 9g (Saturated Fat 1.5g, Trans Fat 0g); Cholesterol 0mg; Sodium 200mg; Total Carbohydrate 2g (Dietary Fiber 0g); Protein 0g **CARBOHYDRATE CHOICES:** 0

Betty's Kitchen Tip If marinating just 1 pound boneless meat or poultry, fish or seafood, use half the marinade as directed above. The remaining marinade can be covered and refrigerated up to 4 days. If you like, toss remaining marinade with fresh vegetables or potatoes and let stand 30 minutes before cooking. Or use some of the remaining marinade to get a jump on other recipes, such as Fish-Cauliflower Cakes with Easy Tartar Sauce (page 262).

Prepared sauces such as barbecue sauce can be hidden sources of sodium. By making your own, you can control how much salt gets added. We've kept the salt low by bulking up this sauce with fresh strawberries and spices for a delicious version. Use it as a sandwich spread or as a glaze or condiment for cooked chicken, beef or pork.

CARB CHOICES

1

Strawberry Barbecue Sauce

PREP TIME: 40 Minutes / **START TO FINISH:** 40 Minutes / *8 servings (2 tablespoons each)*

1 cup coarsely chopped fresh strawberries

½ cup low-salt ketchup

2 tablespoons balsamic vinegar

1 tablespoon packed brown sugar

1 tablespoon yellow mustard

¼ teaspoon ground chipotle chile

¼ teaspoon garlic powder

¼ teaspoon onion powder

⅛ teaspoon salt

1 In 1-quart saucepan, stir together all ingredients. Heat to boiling over medium heat, stirring occasionally. Reduce heat to low. Cook uncovered 15 to 20 minutes, stirring occasionally, or until strawberries are soft. Cool 10 minutes.

2 In blender, place sauce. Cover; blend until smooth. Use immediately or store in tightly covered jar in refrigerator up to 1 month.

1 SERVING Calories 80; Total Fat 0g (Saturated Fat 0g, Trans Fat 0g); Cholesterol 0mg; Sodium 80mg; Total Carbohydrate 18g (Dietary Fiber 0g); Protein 0g **CARBOHYDRATE CHOICES: 1**

This flavorful salad dressing tastes delicious on green salads or vegetables, and as a way to dress up cooked whole grains or rice. You could also use it as a marinade for chicken, beef, pork or veggies.

CARB CHOICES

0

Southwestern Vinaigrette

PREP TIME: 5 Minutes / **START TO FINISH:** 5 Minutes / *6 servings* (*2 tablespoons each*)

½ cup red wine vinegar

¼ cup canola oil

2 teaspoons Salt-Free Taco Seasoning Mix (page 40)

⅛ teaspoon salt

In tightly covered container, shake all ingredients. Store in refrigerator and use within 2 weeks. Shake well before using.

1 SERVING Calories 80; Total Fat 9g (Saturated Fat 0.5g, Trans Fat 0g); Cholesterol 0mg; Sodium 60mg; Total Carbohydrate 0g (Dietary Fiber 0g); Protein 0g **CARBOHYDRATE CHOICES:** 0

Sunny Romaine Salad Place bite-size pieces of romaine lettuce on plates. Top with chopped tomato, crumbled feta cheese and sliced olives. Drizzle with vinaigrette.

Summery Corn Salad Toss whole-kernel corn, black beans, finely chopped red onion and chopped cilantro with vinaigrette. If desired, refrigerate at least 1 hour to blend flavors.

Southwestern Vinaigrette and
Summery Corn Salad

The bright red color of this spread will greet you with a cheery "good morning" when you serve it with breakfast. Keep all but the jar you have open in the freezer, so that you can bring one out at a time for just-picked freshness.

CARB CHOICES

0

Fresh Raspberry Fruit Spread

PREP TIME: 20 Minutes / **START TO FINISH:** 24 Hours 20 Minutes / *3½ half-pints*

1 cup monkfruit 1:1 granules sweetener with erythritol

2 tablespoons less-or-no-sugar-needed powdered pectin (from 1.75-oz box)

1½ pounds fresh red raspberries (5 cups)

1 tablespoon fresh lemon juice

1 tablespoon water

1 In small bowl, stir together sweetener and pectin; set aside.

2 In 3-quart saucepan, crush raspberries, lemon juice and water with potato masher. Heat to full rolling boiling over medium heat about 4 to 5 minutes, stirring constantly. Stir in sweetener mixture. Heat to rolling boil; boil 1 minute longer, stirring constantly.

3 Remove from heat, skim foam off top of mixture. Immediately spoon mixture into 4- or 8-ounce canning jars, leaving at least ½-inch headspace. Wipe rims of containers; cover tightly with lids. Let stand at room temperature about 24 hours.

4 Refrigerate up to 3 weeks or freeze up to 12 months. If frozen, thaw spread in refrigerator, and stir before serving.

1 TABLESPOON Calories 10; Total Fat 0g (Saturated Fat 0g, Trans Fat 0g); Cholesterol 0mg; Sodium 0mg; Total Carbohydrate 2g (Dietary Fiber 1g); Protein 0g **CARBOHYDRATE CHOICES:** 0

Blueberry Fruit Spread Prepare as directed— except substitute blueberries for the raspberries.

Scrumptious Breakfasts

The bottom pancakes on your stack might get a tiny bit jealous if you don't save some of your portion of compote for them. Add another layer of flavor by sprinkling these irresistible pancakes and compote with a pinch of ground nutmeg.

CARB CHOICES

2

Whole Wheat–Oat Pancakes with Raspberry-Apple Compote

PREP TIME: 25 Minutes / **START TO FINISH:** 25 Minutes / *5 servings (3 pancakes and 3 tablespoons compote each)*

RASPBERRY-APPLE COMPOTE

- ½ medium Granny Smith apple, unpeeled, thinly sliced (about 1 cup)
- ½ cup water
- 1 tablespoon packed brown sugar
- 1½ teaspoons cornstarch
- 1 teaspoon fresh lemon juice
- ½ cup fresh raspberries
- ½ teaspoon vanilla

PANCAKES

- 1 egg
- 1 cup white whole wheat flour
- ⅓ cup rolled oats
- 2 teaspoons baking powder
- ¼ teaspoon salt
- 1¼ cups fat-free (skim) milk
- 1 tablespoon canola oil, if needed

1 In 1-quart saucepan, mix all compote ingredients except raspberries and vanilla. Cook over medium-low heat 4 to 5 minutes, stirring occasionally, or until apples are crisp-tender. Remove from heat. Gently stir in raspberries and vanilla; set aside.

2 In medium bowl, beat egg with whisk until well mixed. Stir in remaining pancake ingredients just until flour is moistened. Let stand 1 to 2 minutes to allow batter to thicken.

3 Heat nonstick griddle or skillet over medium-high heat (375°F). Brush with canola oil if necessary to prevent pancakes from sticking to griddle.

4 For each pancake, pour slightly less than ¼ cup batter onto hot griddle. Cook 1 to 2 minutes or until bubbly on top and dry around edges. Turn; cook other side until golden brown. Place pancakes on serving plates. Top pancakes with compote.

1 SERVING Calories 200; Total Fat 5g (Saturated Fat 0.5g, Trans Fat 0g); Cholesterol 40mg; Sodium 350mg; Total Carbohydrate 32g (Dietary Fiber 4g); Protein 7g **CARBOHYDRATE CHOICES:** 2

Betty's Kitchen Tip To test the griddle to see if it's ready, sprinkle with a few drops of water. If bubbles jump around, heat is just right. Make one pancake as a test. If it sticks to the griddle, brush with the oil and heat a minute or two longer before making the remaining pancakes.

Lemon zest is an instant wake-me-up when sprinkled over these yummy waffles. The sunshiny color and the fresh aroma coax you out of sleepiness without saying a word.

Chia Waffles

PREP TIME: 20 Minutes / **START TO FINISH:** 20 Minutes / *4 waffles*

3 eggs
4 egg whites
2 oz (from 8-oz package) ⅓-less-fat cream cheese (Neufchâtel), softened
¼ cup coconut flour

2 tablespoons chia seed
2 teaspoons vanilla
⅛ teaspoon salt
¼ cup Fresh Raspberry Fruit Spread (page 56)
Lemon zest, if desired

1 Heat waffle maker. Waffle makers without a nonstick coating may need to be sprayed with cooking spray before batter for each waffle is added.

2 In medium bowl, beat eggs, egg whites and cream cheese with electric mixer until mixture is almost smooth. Beat in remaining ingredients except fruit spread using whisk.

3 For each waffle, pour scant ½ cup batter into waffle iron. Bake about 2 minutes or until steaming stops. Carefully remove waffle. Serve immediately with fruit spread; sprinkle with lemon zest.

1 WAFFLE Calories 180; Total Fat 10g (Saturated Fat 4g, Trans Fat 0g); Cholesterol 150mg; Sodium 240mg; Total Carbohydrate 9g (Dietary Fiber 5g); Protein 11g **CARBOHYDRATE CHOICES:** ½

Betty's Kitchen Tip The batter will be very thin, but as it cooks it expands and creates a perfect waffle. If you watch the waffle maker during baking, you may notice the lid rise slightly as the waffle bakes.

For an extra punch of fall flavor, sprinkle more pumpkin pie spice over the French toast before serving. Control the amount by placing it in a small spoon or mesh strainer and tapping the handle.

CARB CHOICES

1

Pumpkin Spice French Toast

PREP TIME: 20 Minutes / **START TO FINISH:** 20 Minutes / *6 servings* (*1 slice toast and 2 tablespoons sauce each*)

BROWNED BUTTER–PUMPKIN SAUCE

- 2 **tablespoons butter**
- ⅓ **cup pumpkin (from 15-oz can; not pumpkin pie mix)**
- 3 **tablespoons monkfruit golden 1:1 granules sweetener with erythritol**
- 2 **tablespoons fat-free half-and-half**

FRENCH TOAST

- 2 **eggs**
- 2 **egg whites**
- ⅓ **cup fat-free (skim) milk**
- 2 **teaspoons vanilla**
- 1½ **teaspoons pumpkin pie spice**
- 2 **teaspoons canola oil**
- 6 **slices multigrain bread**

  Additional pumpkin pie spice, if desired

1 In 1-quart saucepan, heat butter over medium-low heat, stirring frequently, just until light brown. Stir in remaining ingredients until smooth. Remove from heat and keep warm.

2 In medium bowl, beat eggs, egg whites, milk, vanilla and pumpkin pie spice with whisk until blended.

3 Brush griddle or large nonstick skillet with canola oil; heat griddle to 350°F or skillet over medium heat. Dip bread slices in egg mixture, coating both sides. Place on griddle. Cook about 4 minutes, turning halfway through cooking, or until golden brown. Serve with Browned Butter–Pumpkin Sauce. Sprinkle with additional pumpkin pie spice.

1 SERVING Calories 180; Total Fat 7g (Saturated Fat 3.5g, Trans Fat 0g); Cholesterol 75mg; Sodium 220mg; Total Carbohydrate 19g (Dietary Fiber 3g); Protein 9g **CARBOHYDRATE CHOICES:** 1

The perfect on-the-go breakfast or snack. The cookies can be frozen in resealable freezer plastic bags for up to 2 months. Take one out on your way out the door to have when you get to your desk. To make it more of a meal, pair it with some protein, such as a hard-cooked egg, low-fat yogurt or a low-fat cheese stick, or something else that fits your healthy eating plan.

CARB CHOICES 1/2

Almond Butter Breakfast Cookies

PREP TIME: 15 Minutes / **START TO FINISH:** 55 Minutes / *About 42 cookies*

½ cup packed brown sugar

½ cup butter, softened

¼ cup almond butter

1 teaspoon vanilla

1 egg

¾ cup white whole wheat flour or whole wheat flour

2 tablespoons ground flax seed

½ teaspoon baking soda

½ teaspoon ground cinnamon

¼ teaspoon ground ginger

1¼ cups old-fashioned oats

¾ cup dried cranberries, dried cherries or dried blueberries

¾ cup chopped toasted almonds

1 Heat oven to 350°F. In large bowl, beat brown sugar, butter, almond butter, vanilla and egg with electric mixer on medium speed until creamy. Stir in flour, flax seed, baking soda, cinnamon and ginger until well blended. Stir in oats, cranberries and almonds.

2 Onto ungreased cookie sheet, drop dough by level measuring tablespoonfuls about 2 inches apart.

3 Bake 7 to 10 minutes or until edges are light golden brown. Cool 2 minutes; remove from cookie sheet to cooling rack. Repeat with remaining dough. To store, cool completely and store tightly covered.

1 COOKIE Calories 90; Total Fat 4.5g (Saturated Fat 1.5g, Trans Fat 0g); Cholesterol 10mg; Sodium 40mg; Total Carbohydrate 9g (Dietary Fiber 1g); Protein 1g **CARBOHYDRATE CHOICES:** ½

Betty's Kitchen Tip To toast almonds, sprinkle in ungreased heavy skillet. Cook over medium-low heat 5 to 7 minutes, stirring frequently or until browning begins, then stirring constantly until golden brown.

If you don't want to bake all the cookies at one time, freeze the dough on cooking parchment paper–lined cookie sheets, then move the frozen cookie dough to a resealable freezer plastic bag. When you're ready to bake, bake as directed, adding a minute or two.

CARB CHOICES

1/2

Butternut Squash Breakfast Cookies

PREP TIME: 20 Minutes / **START TO FINISH:** 1 Hour 35 Minutes / *48 cookies*

½ cup pure maple syrup

½ cup almond butter

¼ cup coconut oil

1 overripe medium banana, mashed

1 box (10 oz) frozen winter squash, cooked as directed on box; cooled

2 eggs

1 teaspoon vanilla

2 cups pure old-fashioned oats

1 cup raisins

½ cup sliced almonds

½ cup unsweetened shredded coconut

1 teaspoon pumpkin pie spice

½ teaspoon salt

½ teaspoon baking soda

1 Heat oven to 375°F. Line two cookie sheets with cooking parchment paper.

2 In large bowl, beat maple syrup, almond butter, oil, mashed banana and cooked squash with electric mixer on medium speed until mixed. Add eggs 1 at a time, beating until mixed. Beat in vanilla. In medium bowl, stir together remaining ingredients. Gradually add to mixture in large bowl, beating after each addition.

3 Onto cookie sheets, drop dough by tablespoonfuls, 3 inches apart.

4 Bake one cookie sheet 18 to 20 minutes or until edges and tops are golden brown. Slide cookies and parchment paper onto cooling rack; cool completely. Repeat with second cookie sheet.

5 Place new piece of cooking parchment paper on each cookie sheet and repeat with remaining dough. To store, place cookies in food storage container with waxed paper or cooking parchment paper between layers; cover and refrigerate.

1 COOKIE Calories 80; Total Fat 4g (Saturated Fat 1.5g, Trans Fat 0g); Cholesterol 10mg; Sodium 45mg; Total Carbohydrate 9g (Dietary Fiber 1g); Protein 1g **CARBOHYDRATE CHOICES:** ½

These yummy muffins can be paired with other foods, such as an egg and fruit, to make a complete meal. Check with your healthcare team on what types of foods you should eat.

CARB CHOICES

1

Almond Flour Zucchini Muffins

PREP TIME: 10 Minutes / **START TO FINISH:** 35 Minutes / *12 muffins*

3 egg whites
1 cup shredded zucchini (about 1 small)
⅓ cup agave nectar
1 cup almond flour
1 cup pure oat flour

2½ teaspoons baking powder
1½ teaspoons pumpkin pie spice
½ teaspoon salt
2 tablespoons sliced almonds

1 Heat oven to 375°F. Place paper baking cup in each of 12 regular-sized muffin cups, or spray cups with cooking spray.

2 In medium bowl, beat egg whites, zucchini and agave with whisk or spoon until well blended. Stir in remaining ingredients except almonds.

3 Divide batter evenly among muffin cups. Sprinkle with almonds.

4 Bake 12 to 15 minutes or until toothpick inserted in center comes out clean. Cool in pan 10 minutes; remove from pan to cooling rack. Serve warm or cool.

1 MUFFIN Calories 140; Total Fat 6g (Saturated Fat 0.5g, Trans Fat 0g); Cholesterol 0mg; Sodium 220mg; Total Carbohydrate 17g (Dietary Fiber 2g); Protein 4g **CARBOHYDRATE CHOICES:** 1

Enjoy these flavorful muffins with a little Fresh Raspberry Fruit Spread (page 56).

CARB CHOICES

1½

Oatmeal–Whole Wheat–Blueberry Muffins

PREP TIME: 15 Minutes / **START TO FINISH:** 40 Minutes / *12 muffins*

1 cup buttermilk

1 cup old-fashioned oats

½ cup packed brown sugar

⅓ cup canola oil

1 egg

½ cup whole wheat flour

½ cup all-purpose flour

1 teaspoon baking soda

1 teaspoon ground cinnamon

¼ teaspoon salt

1 cup fresh or frozen (thawed and drained) blueberries

1 Heat oven to 400°F. Place paper baking cup in each of 12 regular-size muffin cups, or grease bottoms only with shortening or cooking spray.

2 In small bowl, pour buttermilk over oats; set aside. In large bowl, mix brown sugar, oil and egg with spoon. Stir in flours, baking soda, cinnamon and salt just until flours are moistened. Stir in oat mixture. Fold in blueberries. Divide batter evenly among muffin cups.

3 Bake 15 to 20 minutes or until toothpick inserted in center comes out clean. Remove from pan to cooling rack. Serve warm or cool.

1 MUFFIN Calories 180; Total Fat 8g (Saturated Fat 1g, Trans Fat 0g); Cholesterol 15mg; Sodium 180mg; Total Carbohydrate 24g (Dietary Fiber 2g); Protein 3g **CARBOHYDRATE CHOICES:** 1½

If you love pumpkin spice, here's an irresistible way to enjoy it all year long! Freeze cooled muffins in a resealable freezer plastic bag to pull out as many as you want at a time. They will thaw on the counter in about the time it takes to brew some coffee or tea.

CARB CHOICES
1½

Pumpkin Muffins

PREP TIME: 15 Minutes / **START TO FINISH:** 45 Minutes / *24 muffins*

1½ cups whole wheat flour

1 cup all-purpose flour

1½ teaspoons baking soda

¾ teaspoon kosher (coarse) salt

1¼ teaspoons ground cinnamon

1⅛ teaspoons ground nutmeg

¾ teaspoon ground cloves

½ teaspoon ground ginger

1½ cups sugar

⅔ cup canola oil

½ cup water

3 eggs

1 can (15 oz) pumpkin (not pumpkin pie mix)

1 Heat oven to 350°F. Place paper baking cup in each of 24 regular-size muffin cups.

2 In large bowl, mix flours, baking soda, salt, cinnamon, nutmeg, cloves and ginger; make well in center of mixture. In medium bowl, stir sugar, oil, water and eggs with whisk. Stir in pumpkin; add to flour mixture, stirring just until moistened. Divide batter evenly among muffin cups.

3 Bake about 25 minutes or until toothpick inserted in center comes out clean. Cool 5 minutes; remove from pans to cooling racks. Serve warm or cool.

1 MUFFIN Calories 170; Total Fat 7g (Saturated Fat 0.5g, Trans Fat 0g); Cholesterol 25mg; Sodium 160mg; Total Carbohydrate 24g (Dietary Fiber 1g); Protein 2g **CARBOHYDRATE CHOICES:** 1½

Serve these lemon-blueberry scones warm for a tasty breakfast or afternoon treat.

CARB
CHOICES
1½

Lemon-Blueberry Yogurt Scones

PREP TIME: 20 Minutes / **START TO FINISH:** 40 Minutes / *12 scones*

- 2 cups all-purpose flour
- ¼ cup granulated sugar
- 2 teaspoons baking powder
- ¼ teaspoon salt
- ¼ cup cold butter, cut into pieces

- 1 egg white, beaten
- 1 container (6 oz) light very vanilla yogurt
- 1 tablespoon lemon zest
- 1¼ cups blueberries
- 1 tablespoon coarse sugar

1 Heat oven to 400°F. Line cookie sheet with cooking parchment paper.

2 In medium bowl, mix flour, granulated sugar, baking powder and salt. Using pastry blender, cut in butter until mixture looks like coarse crumbs. Stir in egg white, yogurt and lemon zest. Gently stir in blueberries.

3 On lightly floured surface, knead dough 10 to 12 times or until dough is smooth. Pat dough into 7-inch circle. Cut into 12 wedges.

4 Separate wedges and place on cookie sheet. Sprinkle with coarse sugar. Bake 16 to 18 minutes or until golden brown. Immediately transfer from cookie sheet to cooling rack. Cool 5 minutes. Serve warm.

1 SCONE Calories 150; Total Fat 4g (Saturated Fat 2.5g, Trans Fat 0g); Cholesterol 10mg; Sodium 170mg; Total Carbohydrate 25g (Dietary Fiber 1g); Protein 3g **CARBOHYDRATE CHOICES:** 1½

CARBOHYDRATE COUNTING

Carbohydrates Matter

Carbohydrates (frequently referred to as carbs) are your body's preferred way to get energy. The Dietary Guidelines for Americans recommend roughly half of your daily calorie intake should come from carbohydrate foods. When foods that contain carbohydrates are digested, many are broken down into glucose, which raises the level of blood glucose (also called blood sugar) in your body. Your body uses glucose as the "gas" that keeps you running all day. Your pancreas releases insulin to help your cells absorb the glucose.

Carbohydrates often have the biggest impact on your blood sugar levels. If you are living with diabetes, your body either isn't producing enough insulin, or isn't efficiently using the insulin to manage all the glucose you're producing. Left untreated, high blood glucose can lead to health complications. Contrary to popular thinking, people living with diabetes can often enjoy moderate amounts of carbohydrates in their diets.

Why Count Carbs?

Keeping track of the carbohydrates you eat throughout the day by counting carbs can help manage your blood sugar by evenly distributing your carbohydrate calories. Distributing your carbohydrate calories during the day means you can fit a wide variety of foods into your meal plan, so you won't get bored always eating the same foods—yum to that! Your healthcare team may have you count carbs and test your glucose level after you eat to help determine which foods can fit into your meal plan.

How to Count Carbs

Carbs can be counted by one of two methods: the traditional method of counting carbohydrates in a serving, or a simplified version that uses "carbohydrate choices," where one choice represents about 15 grams of carbs. Choose the method that is the easiest for you to follow, and that your healthcare team has discussed with you and approved. The amount of carbs you eat in a day to stay in your target blood sugar range will be different for each person and depends on your age, weight, activity level and other factors.

You can find both the amount of carbohydrates and the number of carbohydrate choices per serving in the recipes in this book. You can also locate the amount of carbohydrates per serving in the Nutrition Facts on packaged products. It's important to pay attention to portion sizes.

Equivalents for Carbohydrate Choices *Use the total carbohydrates listed on the recipe nutrition or nutrition label for a serving*	15 grams total carbs	30 grams total carbs	**Example of Snack Carbohydrates*** 45 grams total carbs
Counting Carbohydrate Choices *Carbohydrate choices are included on the recipes in this book and on other recipes and products. If not available, calculate from food labels by dividing the total carbohydrates by 15.*	1 carb choice	2 carb choices	3 carb choices

*Be sure to check with your diabetes healthcare team to determine the appropriate types and amounts of carbs for you.

What Foods Have Carbs?

Many different foods contain carbohydrates. The goal is to choose nutrient-dense carbohydrates—those foods rich in fiber, vitamins and minerals yet low in added sugars, sodium and unhealthy fats.

Carbs can be found as:

Sugars: naturally occurring sugars such as those in milk or fruit, or sugars added to foods such as soda, cookies and many other packaged foods; can raise blood sugar

Starches: foods high in starch include grains, peas, corn, rice and dried beans; raises blood sugar

Fiber: the part of whole-grain foods and other plant foods that isn't digested; doesn't raise blood sugar

WHAT CARBOHYDRATES SHOULD I EAT?

Eat Plenty	**Non-Starchy Vegetables, Legumes** High in fiber and low in carbs
Eat Some	**Fruits, Whole Grains, Starchy Vegetables, Low-Fat Dairy, Nuts** Contain some carbs and some fiber
Eat Occasionally	**Foods with Added Sugar, such as Baked Goods and Candy or Processed Snacks** Contain lots of carbs and little fiber

Here's a delicious recipe to make ahead and have on hand to grab for quick breakfasts. Just top them before serving and then dig right in!

CARB CHOICES

2

Chocolate-Banana Overnight Oats

PREP TIME: 15 Minutes / **START TO FINISH:** 8 Hours 15 Minutes / *4 servings*

1 cup pure old-fashioned oats

4 teaspoons chia seed

1 square 72% cacao vegan dark chocolate (from 3.5-oz bar), coarsely chopped

1¾ cups unsweetened vanilla almond milk

2 small bananas

2 tablespoons sliced almonds

1 Divide oats evenly among 4 (8-oz) jars or glasses. Divide chia seed and then chocolate among jars.

2 Add milk to jars, dividing evenly; stir.

3 Cover; refrigerate at least 8 hours but no longer than 3 days.

4 For two servings, mash ⅓ of 1 banana. Divide mashed banana evenly between 2 jars of oat mixture; stir. Slice the remaining ⅔ of banana. Top banana-oat mixture with banana slices and 1½ teaspoons of the sliced almonds each. When ready to serve remaining 2 jars, repeat with remaining jars of oat mixture, banana and almond slices.

1 SERVING Calories 220; Total Fat 8g (Saturated Fat 2.5g, Trans Fat 0g); Cholesterol 0mg; Sodium 80mg; Total Carbohydrate 31g (Dietary Fiber 6g); Protein 5g **CARBOHYDRATE CHOICES:** 2

Betty's Kitchen Tip Half-pint (8-oz) canning jars with tight-fitting lids make great jars to make and serve this on-the-run breakfast. For breakfast at home, you can use clear glasses or bowls and cover them with plastic wrap to refrigerate, if you prefer.

The terrific pairing of delicious flavors and textures in this bowl makes breakfast an adventure!

CARB CHOICES 2½

Gingersnap Apple Crisp Yogurt Bowl

PREP TIME: 10 Minutes **/ START TO FINISH:** 10 Minutes **/** *1 serving*

1 container (5.3 oz) vanilla fat-free Greek yogurt

⅓ cup chopped apple

2 tablespoons chopped gingersnap cookies

1 tablespoon toasted coarsely chopped pecans

1 teaspoon pure maple syrup

In small serving bowl, place yogurt. Top with apple, cookies and pecans. Drizzle with maple syrup.

1 SERVING Calories 280; Total Fat 7g (Saturated Fat 1g, Trans Fat 0g); Cholesterol 5mg; Sodium 140mg; Total Carbohydrate 38g (Dietary Fiber 3g); Protein 14g **CARBOHYDRATE CHOICES:** 2½

Betty's Kitchen Tip Try fresh pear in place of the apple.

Betty's Kitchen Tip Share the fun! You can easily double or triple the recipe for additional servings.

Too sleepy to follow a recipe in the morning? The night before, make the cottage cheese mixture, prepare the fresh fruit and place in the serving bowls; cover and refrigerate. Mix the dried fruit–nut mixture and store at room temperature until ready to serve. In the morning, simply add the fruit-nut mixture to the bowls . . . breakfast is ready to devour!

CARB CHOICES

1

Cottage Cheese Breakfast Bowls

PREP TIME: 10 Minutes / **START TO FINISH:** 10 Minutes / *2 servings*

1 cup 2% reduced-fat cottage cheese

¼ teaspoon orange zest

Dash pepper

1 kiwifruit, peeled and sliced

¼ cup fresh blueberries

2 tablespoons pomegranate seeds or unsweetened dried cranberries

2 tablespoons roasted unsalted hulled pumpkin seeds (pepitas)

2 tablespoons chopped walnuts

1 In small bowl, mix cottage cheese, orange zest and pepper. Divide between 2 serving bowls.

2 Divide remaining ingredients between bowls.

1 SERVING Calories 230; Total Fat 11g (Saturated Fat 2.5g, Trans Fat 0g); Cholesterol 15mg; Sodium 350mg; Total Carbohydrate 17g (Dietary Fiber 3g); Protein 16g **CARBOHYDRATE CHOICES:** 1

This hearty, flavorful dish is equally delicious for dinner or breakfast.

CARB CHOICES 4

Spiced Lentil Breakfast Bowls

PREP TIME: 40 Minutes / **START TO FINISH:** 45 Minutes / *4 servings*

LENTILS
- 1¾ cups water
- ½ cup dried lentils, sorted, rinsed

VEGETABLES
- 1 teaspoon olive oil
- 1 cup 1-inch cubes dark-orange sweet potato (1 medium)
- ½ cup chopped green bell pepper
- 1 small onion, chopped (½ cup)
- 1 clove garlic, finely chopped
- 1 can (14.5 oz) no-salt-added diced tomatoes, undrained

- ½ cup raisins
- 2 teaspoons curry powder
- ½ teaspoon ground cumin
- ½ teaspoon chili powder
- ¼ teaspoon salt

TOPPINGS AND SERVE-WITHS
- 4 eggs
- 1 tablespoon chopped fresh cilantro
- 4 slices whole-grain toast

1 In 1½-quart saucepan, heat water and lentils over high heat to boiling. Reduce heat, cover and simmer 15 to 17 minutes, stirring occasionally, or until lentils just begin to soften.

2 In 10-inch nonstick skillet, heat oil over medium heat until hot. Add sweet potato, bell pepper, onion and garlic; cook uncovered 4 minutes, stirring frequently. Stir in lentils and cooking liquid, tomatoes, raisins, curry powder, cumin, chili powder and salt. Heat to boiling, stirring occasionally. Reduce heat; simmer 9 to 12 minutes or until sweet potatoes and lentils are tender.

3 Meanwhile, in 10-inch skillet or 2-quart saucepan, heat 2 to 3 inches water to boiling. Reduce heat so water is simmering. Break 1 egg into custard cup or small glass bowl. Holding it close to the water's edge, carefully slide it into the water. Repeat with remaining eggs. Cook uncovered 3 to 5 minutes or until whites and yolks are firm, not runny. Remove from water with a slotted spoon.

4 For each serving, spoon about 1 cup lentil mixture into bowl or onto plate. Top with a poached egg and sprinkle with cilantro. Serve with toast.

1 SERVING Calories 390; Total Fat 8g (Saturated Fat 2g, Trans Fat 0g); Cholesterol 185mg; Sodium 430mg; Total Carbohydrate 59g (Dietary Fiber 10g); Protein 19g **CARBOHYDRATE CHOICES:** 4

Make Ahead Prepare the lentil-vegetable mixture. Cover; store in the refrigerator up to 5 days. Reheat just before serving.

Make these quick little egg dishes new each time by experimenting with different veggies or cheese, such as different color bell peppers, finely chopped yellow squash or broccoli florets or crumbled feta cheese instead of goat cheese.

CARB CHOICES

0

Mini Veggie Frittatas

PREP TIME: 20 Minutes / **START TO FINISH:** 45 Minutes / *6 servings (2 frittatas each)*

6 eggs

3 egg whites

½ cup chopped red bell pepper

¼ cup chopped poblano chile

¼ cup finely chopped zucchini

¼ cup crumbled goat cheese (1 oz)

¼ cup fat-free (skim) milk

¼ teaspoon salt

¼ teaspoon pepper

4 green onions, thinly sliced (¼ cup)

2 cloves garlic, finely chopped

Chopped green onion, if desired

1 Heat oven to 350°F. Spray 12 regular-size muffin cups with cooking spray.

2 In medium bowl, beat eggs and egg whites with fork or whisk until well mixed. Stir in remaining ingredients until well blended. Divide egg mixture evenly among muffin cups.

3 Bake about 25 minutes or until knife inserted in center comes out clean. Let stand 5 minutes. Run knife around edge of each frittata; remove gently with fork. Sprinkle with chopped green onion. Serve immediately.

1 SERVING Calories 120; Total Fat 7g (Saturated Fat 2.5g, Trans Fat 0g); Cholesterol 190mg; Sodium 210mg; Total Carbohydrate 4g (Dietary Fiber 0g); Protein 10g **CARBOHYDRATE CHOICES:** 0

Betty's Kitchen Tip When serving these cute little frittatas, you can finely chop any leftover poblano chile or slice extra green onions to sprinkle over the top.

Make these quick little egg dishes new each time by experimenting with different veggies or cheese, such as different color bell peppers, finely chopped yellow squash or broccoli florets or crumbled feta cheese instead of goat cheese.

CARB CHOICES

0

Mini Veggie Frittatas

PREP TIME: 20 Minutes / **START TO FINISH:** 45 Minutes / *6 servings (2 frittatas each)*

6 eggs

3 egg whites

½ cup chopped red bell pepper

¼ cup chopped poblano chile

¼ cup finely chopped zucchini

¼ cup crumbled goat cheese (1 oz)

¼ cup fat-free (skim) milk

¼ teaspoon salt

¼ teaspoon pepper

4 green onions, thinly sliced (¼ cup)

2 cloves garlic, finely chopped

Chopped green onion, if desired

1 Heat oven to 350°F. Spray 12 regular-size muffin cups with cooking spray.

2 In medium bowl, beat eggs and egg whites with fork or whisk until well mixed. Stir in remaining ingredients until well blended. Divide egg mixture evenly among muffin cups.

3 Bake about 25 minutes or until knife inserted in center comes out clean. Let stand 5 minutes. Run knife around edge of each frittata; remove gently with fork. Sprinkle with chopped green onion. Serve immediately.

1 SERVING Calories 120; Total Fat 7g (Saturated Fat 2.5g, Trans Fat 0g); Cholesterol 190mg; Sodium 210mg; Total Carbohydrate 4g (Dietary Fiber 0g); Protein 10g **CARBOHYDRATE CHOICES:** 0

Betty's Kitchen Tip When serving these cute little frittatas, you can finely chop any leftover poblano chile or slice extra green onions to sprinkle over the top.

There's a new toast in town! Caramelized sweet potato planks make a delicious substitute for bread, topped with leafy kale, savory prosciutto and a tart, creamy sauce.

Sweet Potato Toast with Kale and Prosciutto

PREP TIME: 15 Minutes / **START TO FINISH:** 40 Minutes / *4 servings*

4 (¼-inch thick) lengthwise slices dark-orange sweet potato

5 teaspoons olive oil

¼ teaspoon smoked paprika

¼ teaspoon salt

¼ teaspoon pepper

2 cups chopped fresh kale leaves (ribs removed)

¼ cup thinly sliced red onion

¼ cup plain Greek yogurt

1 tablespoon lemon juice

1½ slices prosciutto, torn into 1-inch-wide strips

1 Heat oven to 425°F. Brush both sides of sweet potato slices with 2 teaspoons of the olive oil; place on ungreased cookie sheet. Sprinkle with paprika and ⅛ teaspoon of the salt. Bake 15 to 20 minutes, turning once, or until golden brown.

2 Meanwhile, in medium bowl, mix 2 teaspoons of the olive oil, remaining ⅛ teaspoon salt and the pepper. Add kale and onion; toss to coat.

3 Divide kale mixture evenly over sweet potato toasts. Bake 4 to 5 minutes longer or until kale wilts slightly.

4 Meanwhile, in small bowl, stir together yogurt, remaining 1 teaspoon olive oil and the lemon juice.

5 Place toasts on serving plates; drizzle with yogurt mixture and top with prosciutto.

1 SERVING Calories 190; Total Fat 7g (Saturated Fat 1.5g, Trans Fat 0g); Cholesterol 0mg; Sodium 280mg; Total Carbohydrate 28g (Dietary Fiber 4g); Protein 4g **CARBOHYDRATE CHOICES:** 2

Betty's Kitchen Tip Leaving the skin on the sweet potato makes the slices sturdier for turning and transferring to plates.

Betty's Kitchen Tip To take the harsh edge off red onion, place the sliced onion in a strainer and rinse under cold water 30 seconds, then pat dry before using.

You'll love this delicious new way to enjoy scrambled eggs. These toasts are hearty, beautiful and bursting with flavor.

Scrambled Egg and Veggie Toast

PREP TIME: 30 Minutes / **START TO FINISH:** 30 Minutes / *4 toasts*

- 2 100% whole wheat sandwich thins
- 1 teaspoon olive oil
- 1 small zucchini, cut in half lengthwise, then cut crosswise into thin slices (¾ cup)
- ¼ cup thinly sliced red onion
- ⅓ cup sliced cherry tomatoes
- 1 tablespoon thinly sliced fresh basil leaves

- 3 eggs
- 3 tablespoons water
- ¼ cup reduced-fat garden vegetable cream cheese spread (from 7.5-oz container)
- ¼ cup shredded reduced-fat mozzarella cheese (1 oz)

  Additional thinly sliced fresh basil leaves, if desired

1 Heat oven to 350°F. Separate each sandwich thin horizontally. On cookie sheet, place sandwich thins cut side up. Bake 8 to 10 minutes or until toasted.

2 Meanwhile, in 10-inch nonstick skillet, heat oil over medium heat. Add zucchini and onion; cook 2 to 4 minutes, stirring frequently, or until tender. Remove from heat; stir in tomatoes and basil. Remove from skillet to heatproof plate; cover with foil to keep warm.

3 In small bowl, beat eggs and water with fork or whisk until well mixed. Heat same skillet over medium-low heat; pour in egg mixture. As egg mixture begins to set at bottom and side, gently lift cooked portions so that thin, uncooked portion can flow to bottom. Avoid constant stirring. Cook 3 to 4 minutes or until eggs are thickened throughout but still moist.

4 Spread each sandwich thin half with 1 tablespoon cream cheese. Divide eggs evenly on top of cream cheese; top with vegetable mixture and sprinkle with mozzarella cheese.

5 Bake 3 to 5 minutes or just until mozzarella cheese is melted. Garnish with additional basil; serve immediately.

1 TOAST Calories 360; Total Fat 11g (Saturated Fat 4g, Trans Fat 0g); Cholesterol 155mg; Sodium 250mg; Total Carbohydrate 55g (Dietary Fiber 6g); Protein 10g **CARBOHYDRATE CHOICES:** 3½

Betty's Kitchen Tip To cut thin strips of basil or other leafy herbs easily, start by stacking the leaves. Roll up the stack lengthwise into a tight cylinder, then cut roll crosswise into thin slices.

Betty's Kitchen Tip If you like, substitute reduced-fat plain cream cheese spread or reduced-fat chives-and-onion cream cheese spread for the garden vegetable cream cheese.

This falls in the "I can't believe I get to eat this!" category. It's a scrumptious mash-up of avocado toast meets breakfast pizza. And meatballs for breakfast? We call that fun on a plate.

CARB CHOICES

1

Savory Breakfast Tartines

PREP TIME: 15 Minutes / **START TO FINISH:** 15 Minutes / *4 servings*

1 small ripe avocado

1 teaspoon fresh lemon juice

⅛ teaspoon salt

⅛ teaspoon pepper

2 sprouted whole-grain English muffins, split

6 Freezer-Friendly Turkey Meatballs (page 25), thawed

2 tablespoons shredded reduced-fat cheddar cheese

3 tablespoons coarsely chopped grape tomatoes

2 teaspoons chopped Italian (flat-leaf) parsley

1 Cut avocado lengthwise in half; remove pit and peel. In small bowl, mash avocado with fork; stir in lemon juice, salt and pepper.

2 Toast English muffin halves.

3 Meanwhile, cut each meatball in half. In small microwavable bowl, place meatball halves; cover with plastic wrap. Microwave on High 1 minute or until heated through.

4 Divide avocado mixture evenly among muffin halves; spread to within ¼ inch of edge. Place 3 meatball halves, cut side down, on each muffin half. Sprinkle with cheese, tomatoes and parsley. Serve immediately.

1 SERVING Calories 210; Total Fat 10g (Saturated Fat 2g, Trans Fat 0g); Cholesterol 35mg; Sodium 370mg; Total Carbohydrate 20g (Dietary Fiber 5g); Protein 11g **CARBOHYDRATE CHOICES: 1**

These handheld filled tortillas make it easy to eat breakfast on the go. You can make them ahead and reheat just before you head out the door!

CARB CHOICES
1

Freezer Breakfast Tortilla Stacks

PREP TIME: 20 Minutes / **START TO FINISH:** 30 Minutes / *8 servings*

⅓ cup Make-Ahead Mexican-Style Turkey Sausage (page 30)

⅓ cup no-salt pinto beans (from 15-oz can), rinsed, drained

8 (6-inch) low-carb whole wheat or multigrain tortillas

½ cup Make-Ahead Cilantro-Lime Barley (page 34)

2 oz reduced-fat pepper Jack or Monterey Jack cheese, shredded (½ cup)

4 teaspoons chopped fresh cilantro

½ cup pico de gallo (for homemade pico de gallo, see page 42)

1 Heat oven to 350°F. In small bowl, stir together turkey sausage and beans.

2 Make one cut in each tortilla from edge to center. Onto each tortilla, spoon 1 tablespoon of the barley over the tortilla quarter to the left of the cut. Sprinkle 1 tablespoon cheese and ½ teaspoon cilantro over the tortilla quarter above barley. Spoon 1 tablespoon pico de gallo over tortilla quarter next to the cheese. Spoon generous 1 tablespoon meat-bean mixture on remaining quarter of the tortilla.

3 Starting with barley-covered section, fold tortilla quarter and filling up and over the adjacent section, folding in a clockwise direction until a wedge-shaped stack is formed.

4 On ungreased 15×10×1-inch pan, arrange tortilla stacks. Bake about 10 minutes or until tortillas are hot and cheese is melted.

5 Serve warm. Or cool completely and wrap tortilla stacks individually in foil. Freeze up to 6 months. To reheat, remove foil and place frozen tortilla stack on microwavable plate. Microwave uncovered on High for 1 minute or until fillings are hot, turning halfway through cooking.

1 SERVING Calories 120; Total Fat 3.5g (Saturated Fat 1g, Trans Fat 0g); Cholesterol 10mg; Sodium 240mg; Total Carbohydrate 17g (Dietary Fiber 2g); Protein 5g **CARBOHYDRATE CHOICES: 1**

Betty's Kitchen Tip The quickest way to assemble these is to set out all the tortillas on your work surface, top with ingredients and then fold them up.

You can add the leftover black beans to salads, to rice, grain or pasta dishes or to scrambled eggs.

CARB CHOICES

2

Southwestern-Style Breakfast Tostadas

PREP TIME: 10 Minutes / **START TO FINISH:** 20 Minutes / *2 servings*

2 (6-inch) corn tortillas

½ cup black beans, rinsed, drained (from 15-oz can)

½ cup fat-free egg product

1 tablespoon fat-free (skim) milk

⅛ teaspoon pepper
Dash salt

½ cup chopped tomato

2 tablespoons crumbled queso fresco or shredded Monterey Jack cheese

2 teaspoons chopped fresh cilantro

2 tablespoons fat-free Greek yogurt

1 Warm tortillas as directed on package. Meanwhile, in small bowl, use potato masher or fork to slightly mash beans; set aside.

2 In another small bowl or 1-cup glass measure, mix egg product, milk, pepper and salt. Beat with fork until well blended.

3 Heat 8-inch nonstick skillet over medium heat. Pour egg product mixture into skillet. Cook, without stirring, until egg mixture begins to set. Run spatula around edge of skillet, lifting egg product mixture so uncooked portion flows underneath. Continue cooking about 2 minutes more or until egg product mixture is cooked but still moist. Remove from heat.

4 Spread 1 tortilla with the beans. Top with the remaining tortilla, cooked egg product mixture, tomato, cheese and 1 teaspoon of the cilantro. Cut in half to serve. If desired, fold each portion in half. Top with yogurt and remaining cilantro.

1 SERVING Calories 190; Total Fat 3g (Saturated Fat 1g, Trans Fat 0g); Cholesterol 5mg; Sodium 440mg; Total Carbohydrate 26g (Dietary Fiber 7g); Protein 15g **CARBOHYDRATE CHOICES:** 2

Tasty
Light Meals
& Snacks

Sprouted grain bread is made from whole grains that were allowed to germinate (sprout) before being milled into flour.

Skinny Chicken and Roasted Vegetable Panini

PREP TIME: 45 Minutes / **START TO FINISH:** 45 Minutes / *2 panini*

4 teaspoons red wine vinegar

1 teaspoon olive oil

⅛ teaspoon salt

1 zucchini, cut lengthwise into thin slices

2 (¼-inch-thick) slices red onion

1 medium tomato, cut crosswise into 4 slices

1 small red bell pepper

4 slices sprouted wheat bread

¼ cup shredded deli rotisserie chicken breast (from 2-lb chicken)

¼ cup lightly packed fresh basil leaves

¼ cup shredded reduced-fat mozzarella cheese (1 oz)

1 Heat oven to 450°F. Line 2 cookie sheets with foil; spray with cooking spray.

2 In small bowl, mix vinegar, olive oil and salt.

3 Using pastry brush, brush zucchini and onion with vinegar mixture; reserve remaining mixture. Place zucchini and onion in single layer on one of the cookie sheets. Place tomato slices on second cookie sheet. Roast vegetables 25 to 30 minutes or until zucchini and onion are golden brown, turning vegetables and rotating pans after about 15 minutes.

4 Meanwhile, roast bell pepper over open gas flame or under broiler until blackened on all sides. Transfer to medium bowl; cover with plastic wrap. Let stand 5 minutes. Remove skin, stem, seeds and membranes from pepper. Cut pepper into 1-inch strips.

5 Spray contact grill or panini maker with cooking spray. Heat closed grill 3 to 5 minutes or according to directions.

6 Divide vegetables between 2 of the bread slices. Brush remaining vinegar mixture over veggies. Top with chicken, basil and cheese. Top with second slice of bread. When grill is heated, place panini in grill. Close grill; grill 4 to 5 minutes or until cheese is melted and bread is thoroughly toasted.

1 PANINI Calories 300; Total Fat 7g (Saturated Fat 0.5g, Trans Fat 0g); Cholesterol 20mg; Sodium 470mg; Total Carbohydrate 40g (Dietary Fiber 8g); Protein 19g **CARBOHYDRATE CHOICES:** 2½

Betty's Kitchen Tip Look for sprouted 100% whole-grain bread in the bakery or freezer section of your local grocery store.

This is a wonderful soup to prepare when it's cold outside. The winter root vegetables don't take long to cook, but the heartwarming flavors will make you think it's been simmering all day.

CARB CHOICES
1½

Root Vegetable Chicken Soup

PREP TIME: 25 Minutes / **START TO FINISH:** 40 Minutes / *6 servings*

2 tablespoons butter

3 medium carrots, thinly sliced (1 cup)

3 medium parsnips, peeled, thinly sliced (1 cup)

2 medium leeks, cut in half lengthwise, rinsed and cut crosswise into ½-inch pieces (2 cups)

4 cups reduced-sodium chicken broth (for homemade broth, see page 12)

⅓ cup uncooked orzo or rosamarina pasta (2 oz)

2 cups chopped cooked chicken (for homemade chicken, see page 12)

2 tablespoons chopped fresh or 2 teaspoons dried dill weed

1 In 4-quart saucepan, melt butter over medium heat. Cook carrots, parsnips and leeks in butter 3 to 5 minutes, stirring occasionally, or until carrots and parsnips are crisp-tender.

2 Stir in broth and pasta. Heat to boiling; reduce heat to low. Cover; simmer 10 to 12 minutes, stirring occasionally, or until pasta is tender.

3 Stir in chicken and dill; cook until thoroughly heated.

1 SERVING Calories 230; Total Fat 9g (Saturated Fat 4g, Trans Fat 0g); Cholesterol 45mg; Sodium 260mg; Total Carbohydrate 24g (Dietary Fiber 4g); Protein 13g **CARBOHYDRATE CHOICES:** 1½

Betty's Kitchen Tip Soup gets even more flavorful after the flavors have had a chance to mingle. If it gets too thick after heating, add a tablespoon of water to thin it back out to the desired consistency.

Tuck some slices of cucumber into these pockets for some extra crunch, if you like.

CARB CHOICES 1½

Greek-Style Turkey Burgers with Cucumber Sauce

PREP TIME: 20 Minutes / **START TO FINISH:** 30 Minutes / *4 burgers*

CUCUMBER SAUCE

- ⅓ cup plain fat-free yogurt
- ⅓ cup chopped cucumber
- 1½ teaspoons chopped fresh mint leaves
- ¾ teaspoon fresh lemon juice

BURGERS

- 1 box (9 oz) frozen chopped spinach
- 1 lb ground turkey (at least 93% lean)

- 3 tablespoons plain fat-free yogurt
- 1 teaspoon dried oregano leaves, crushed
- ½ teaspoon garlic salt
- ¼ teaspoon pepper
- 4 thin slices medium tomato, halved
- 2 whole-grain pita (pocket) breads (6-inch), cut in half to form pockets

1 Set oven control to broil. In medium bowl, stir together cucumber sauce ingredients; cover and refrigerate until ready to use.

2 Cook spinach as directed on box; cool slightly. Squeeze to drain well. In large bowl, mix spinach and remaining ingredients except for tomato and pitas. Shape into 4 oval patties, about ½ inch thick. On broiler pan, place patties. Broil with tops about 5 inches from heat 10 to 12 minutes, turning once, or until instant-read meat thermometer inserted in center of burgers reads 165°F.

3 Place 2 tomato slice halves in each pita pocket half; place burgers over tomato slices. To serve, top each burger with about 3 tablespoons sauce.

1 BURGER Calories 300; Total Fat 11g (Saturated Fat 2.5g, Trans Fat 0g); Cholesterol 85mg; Sodium 380mg; Total Carbohydrate 22g (Dietary Fiber 4g); Protein 29g **CARBOHYDRATE CHOICES:** 1½

Betty's Kitchen Tip You can use a contact grill for these burgers. Heat closed medium-size contact grill for 5 minutes. Position drip tray to catch drippings. When grill is heated, place burgers on grill. Close grill; cook 4 to 6 minutes or until instant-read meat thermometer inserted in center of burgers reads 165°F.

These fish tacos feature a creamy, tangy crema that doubles as a dressing for the slaw.

Fish Tacos with Herbed Crema

PREP TIME: 35 Minutes / **START TO FINISH:** 35 Minutes / *8 servings*

HERBED CREMA AND SLAW

1⅓	cups plain low-fat Greek yogurt
¼	cup chopped fresh cilantro
2	tablespoons fresh lime juice
¼	teaspoon salt
2	cloves garlic, finely chopped
3	cups shredded green cabbage

TACOS

4	(4-oz) skinless white fish fillets (halibut or mahi mahi), about ¾ inch thick
1	tablespoon olive oil
¼	teaspoon salt
¼	teaspoon black pepper
¼	teaspoon ground red pepper (cayenne)
8	(6-inch) corn tortillas, heated as directed on package
½	cup thinly sliced radishes
1	lime, cut into wedges

1 In medium bowl, stir together yogurt, cilantro, lime juice, ¼ teaspoon salt and garlic. In another medium bowl, toss cabbage and ½ cup of the yogurt mixture until evenly coated. Refrigerate remaining yogurt mixture.

2 Place oven rack 4 inches from broiler. Set oven control to broil. Brush both sides of fish with olive oil. Sprinkle both sides with salt, black pepper and red pepper. Place on ungreased cookie sheet. Broil 7 to 10 minutes, turning once, or until fish flakes easily with fork. Cool slightly. Flake fish into bite-size pieces.

3 Divide cabbage mixture evenly among tortillas. Top with fish and radishes. Spoon 2 tablespoons of the remaining yogurt mixture over fish on each taco. Serve with lime wedges.

1 SERVING Calories 160; Total Fat 4g (Saturated Fat 1g, Trans Fat 0g); Cholesterol 30mg; Sodium 220mg; Total Carbohydrate 16g (Dietary Fiber 2g); Protein 16g **CARBOHYDRATE CHOICES:** 1

Betty's Kitchen Tip To save time, use shredded cabbage from the produce section.

Serving salmon as burgers is an economical way to enjoy this flavorful fish. Adding delicious Asian seasonings and a lightened-up sauce will make this feel like a fancy restaurant meal—but it takes only 45 minutes to get it on the table.

CARB CHOICES

1

Soy-Ginger Salmon Burgers

PREP TIME: 35 Minutes / **START TO FINISH:** 45 Minutes / *4 burgers*

BURGERS
- 1 lb skinless salmon fillet, cut into large cubes
- 2 tablespoons grated gingerroot
- 4 green onions, thinly sliced (¼ cup)
- ⅓ cup plain panko crispy bread crumbs
- 4 teaspoons reduced-sodium soy sauce
- 1 tablespoon olive oil
- 4 large leaves red leaf or Bibb lettuce

- 1 avocado, pitted, peeled and thinly sliced

AIOLI
- ½ cup plain low-fat yogurt
- 1 teaspoon honey
- ½ teaspoon wasabi powder or prepared horseradish
- ¼ teaspoon salt
- 2 cloves garlic, finely chopped

1 Heat oven to 400°F.

2 In food processor, place salmon, gingerroot and green onions. Cover; process using quick on-and-off pulses several times until mixture comes together. In large bowl, place salmon mixture. Add bread crumbs and soy sauce; mix well. Shape mixture into 4 patties, ½- to ¾-inch thick.

3 Heat 10-inch ovenproof skillet or grill pan over medium-high heat. Add oil and patties. Cook 3 minutes; turn patties, and transfer pan to oven. Bake 8 to 10 minutes or until cooked through.

4 Meanwhile, in small bowl, stir together aioli ingredients.

5 Place each burger in a lettuce leaf; top each with 2 tablespoons aioli and avocado slices.

1 BURGER Calories 350; Total Fat 19g (Saturated Fat 3.5g, Trans Fat 0g); Cholesterol 65mg; Sodium 430mg; Total Carbohydrate 16g (Dietary Fiber 3g); Protein 28g **CARBOHYDRATE CHOICES:** 1

Betty's Kitchen Tip Other types of fish, such as tuna, snapper or sea bass, will work equally well in this recipe. Use your favorite or what's on sale.

Betty's Kitchen Tip Wasabi, also called Japanese horseradish, has a sharp, pungent, fiery flavor. It comes in both powder and paste form, and is available in the international food aisle of large supermarkets.

These rolls have fun written all over them. The festive and colorful ingredients are begging to be served at a party or are equally delicious as a snack.

CARB CHOICES 1½

Shrimp Summer Rolls with Dipping Sauce

PREP TIME: 40 Minutes / **START TO FINISH:** 40 Minutes / *12 rolls (1 roll and 1 tablespoon dipping sauce each)*

DIPPING SAUCE
- ½ cup water
- ⅓ cup hoisin sauce (from 7.25-oz jar)
- 1 teaspoon roasted red chili paste (from 4-oz jar)
- ¼ teaspoon crushed red pepper flakes

SUMMER ROLLS
- 4 oz dried thin rice noodles or rice vermicelli (from 8.8-oz package)
- 2 cups shredded romaine lettuce
- ½ cup lightly packed fresh cilantro leaves
- ½ cup shredded carrot (about 1 medium)
- 10 oz frozen cooked salad shrimp (about 1¾ cups), thawed, drained
- 12 (about 8-inch) round rice paper wrappers (from 12-oz package)

1 In medium bowl, mix dipping sauce ingredients. Cover; refrigerate.

2 Cook and drain noodles as directed on package. Meanwhile, in large bowl, mix lettuce, cilantro, carrot and shrimp.

3 Sprinkle water over a paper towel; place on cutting board. Fill a 10-inch pie plate with water. Place 1 rice paper wrapper in water 45 to 60 seconds or until pliable but not completely softened. Gently remove wrapper from water, shaking to drain excess water; place on damp paper towel.

4 Starting close to edge of wrapper closest to you, place a crosswise row of about ¼ cup noodles. On top of noodles, arrange about ⅓ cup of the lettuce mixture. Starting with edge covered with fillings, roll up wrapper over fillings using paper towel to aid rolling, stopping after first turn to tuck in sides. Continue to roll up, tucking in sides. Place roll seam side down on platter.

5 Repeat with remaining wrappers. Do not let rolls touch each other. (If rolls touch, they will stick together.) Serve immediately with sauce, or cover with moist paper towels and refrigerate up to 2 hours. To serve, cut each roll in half diagonally.

1 ROLL Calories 120; Total Fat 1g (Saturated Fat 0g, Trans Fat 0g); Cholesterol 35mg; Sodium 350mg; Total Carbohydrate 23g (Dietary Fiber 1g); Protein 5g **CARBOHYDRATE CHOICES:** 1½

Betty's Kitchen Tip Rice paper, an edible sheet, is made from a dough of rice flour, water and salt. It's great to have on hand to wrap a variety of fillings. Look for rice paper in the international section of the supermarket or at Asian grocery stores.

SMART SNACKING

Snacks Can Be Your Oasis

Many people think following a diabetes-friendly meal plan will leave them hungry and unsatisfied. Not so, if you work healthy snacks into your daily eating plan. Think of them as the little refueling spots that bridge mealtimes so you don't end up overeating. Nutritious snacks can help fill you up and give you a boost of energy.

Use planned snack times as additional ways to boost your intake of veggies, fruits, whole grains and healthy fats while sticking to your daily nutritional requirements. Pairing whole grains with protein and healthy fats can help keep you satisfied. Veggies add bulk and can help fill you up. Check with your healthcare team for what will work for your meal plan. Look at the delicious options in this chapter, as well as in our Sweet Treats & Refreshing Drinks chapter starting on page 281, for scrumptious options that fit the bill no matter what you are yearning for.

Tips for Snacking

Know Why You're Snacking Are you hungry, or are you tired or bored? If you are tired, rest. If you are bored, go for a walk or call a friend. Snack only when you are hungry.

Watch Your Portions Use measuring cups and spoons to help measure foods rather than guessing at the amount.

Snack Without Distractions Don't eat while watching TV, reading or driving. Being intentional about eating will help your brain realize sooner that you are full.

Stock Up Keep healthy snacks in your fridge and pantry, such as veggies cut up and stored in clear containers in the fridge, so you can easily reach for them.

Count the Carbs Be sure to count your snacks toward your daily carbs (see page 78).

CUPS FROM TOP LEFT TO RIGHT:

Top Row: Carrot sticks, blueberries, Chocolate–Peanut Butter Energy Balls (page 146)

Second Row: Grapes, Easy Baked Apple Chips (page 148), cucumber and tomatoes

Third Row: Hard-cooked eggs, Almond Butter–Cranberry Energy Balls (page 146), plain popcorn

Fourth Row: Spicy White Cheddar Mix (page 151), Blueberry-Grape Smoothie Poppers (page 158) and Lime Green Smoothie Poppers (page 159), almonds and bell pepper slices

These gorgeous romaine boats are so pretty to look at and super fun to eat. As you pick one up, you can roll it up or fold in the sides before diving in!

Loaded BLT Avocado Lettuce Wraps

PREP TIME: 25 Minutes / **START TO FINISH:** 25 Minutes / *12 servings*

1 cup diced plum (Roma) tomatoes (2 medium)

1 small yellow onion, diced (½ cup)

1 tablespoon chopped fresh cilantro

2 teaspoons seeded and finely chopped serrano chile (about 1 large)

1 teaspoon fresh lime juice

½ teaspoon salt

12 leaves romaine lettuce hearts

2 ripe medium avocados, pitted, peeled and diced (about 2 cups)

¾ cup diced red bell pepper

6 slices gluten-free bacon, cooked and chopped

1 In small bowl, mix tomatoes, onion, cilantro, chile, lime juice and salt.

2 Arrange lettuce leaves on serving platter. Divide avocados and bell pepper among lettuce leaves. Top with tomato mixture and bacon.

1 SERVING Calories 70; Total Fat 5g (Saturated Fat 1g, Trans Fat 0g); Cholesterol 0mg; Sodium 170mg; Total Carbohydrate 5g (Dietary Fiber 2g); Protein 2g **CARBOHYDRATE CHOICES:** ½

No forks needed! This handheld Greek salad is great for a picnic or casual get-together. Make the sauce and chicken mixture ahead of time, then assemble just before serving.

CARB CHOICES

0

Greek Lettuce Wraps

PREP TIME: 30 Minutes / **START TO FINISH:** 30 Minutes / *12 wraps*

TZATZIKI SAUCE

- ½ cup plain fat-free Greek yogurt
- ⅓ cup finely chopped seeded peeled cucumber
- 2 teaspoons olive oil
- 2 teaspoons fresh lemon juice
- 2 teaspoons chopped fresh dill weed
- 1 clove garlic, finely chopped

WRAPS

- 1½ cups chopped gluten-free deli rotisserie chicken (from 2-lb chicken)
- ½ cup crumbled feta cheese (2 oz)
- ¼ cup finely chopped red onion
- ¼ cup sliced pitted kalamata olives
- 1 medium tomato, seeded, chopped (½ cup)
- 12 large leaves Boston lettuce (from 2 heads)
  Fresh dill sprigs, if desired

1 In small bowl, mix all sauce ingredients. Cover; refrigerate.

2 In medium bowl, mix chicken, cheese, onion, olives and tomato.

3 To serve, spoon scant ¼ cup chicken mixture on each lettuce leaf; top with scant 1 tablespoon sauce. Top with dill sprig.

1 WRAP Calories 70; Total Fat 3.5g (Saturated Fat 1g, Trans Fat 0g); Cholesterol 20mg; Sodium 170mg; Total Carbohydrate 2g (Dietary Fiber 0g); Protein 6g **CARBOHYDRATE CHOICES:** 0

Betty's Kitchen Tip To seed a cucumber, cut the cucumber in half lengthwise. Use a spoon or melon baller to scoop out the seeds that run along the center.

Make Ahead The tzatziki sauce and chicken mixture can be prepared up to 24 hours before serving, which allows for the flavors to blend. Cover; refrigerate in separate covered containers until you're ready to assemble the wraps.

Use cooked chicken from Reduced-Sodium Roasted Chicken and Broth (page 12) or Rotisserie-Style Chicken (page 17), which you've been keeping in the freezer for a recipe like this one, and your salad is just minutes away from being devoured!

CARB CHOICES

1/2

Cobb Salad Lettuce Wraps

PREP TIME: 20 Minutes / **START TO FINISH:** 20 Minutes / *4 servings (2 wraps each)*

- 8 leaves Bibb lettuce
- 1½ cups shredded cooked chicken breast, thawed if frozen
- 1 small avocado, pitted, peeled and thinly sliced
- 1 medium tomato, cut into thin wedges
- ¼ cup finely chopped red onion
- ½ cup light blue cheese dressing
- 1 tablespoon red wine vinegar
- 4 slices gluten-free bacon, crisply cooked, crumbled

1 Place lettuce leaves on plate. Divide chicken among lettuce leaves, placing lengthwise in center. Top with avocado and tomato wedges. Sprinkle with red onion.

2 In small bowl, mix dressing and vinegar. Drizzle over lettuce wraps. Top with crumbled bacon.

1 SERVING Calories 220; Total Fat 13g (Saturated Fat 3g, Trans Fat 0g); Cholesterol 50mg; Sodium 470mg; Total Carbohydrate 6g (Dietary Fiber 3g); Protein 21g **CARBOHYDRATE CHOICES:** ½

Betty's Kitchen Tip In a hurry? Try using precooked bacon. You can heat the bacon quickly in the microwave so it will crumble more easily.

This fix-and-forget recipe makes a delicious and satisfying soup that's perfect for lunch or a light dinner. Fresh thyme leaves make a pretty garnish, if you like to top your soups with "a little something" special.

CARB CHOICES 2

Healthy Split Pea Soup

PREP TIME: 15 Minutes / **START TO FINISH:** 10 Hours 15 Minutes / *8 servings (1½ cups each)*

7 cups water

1 package (16 oz) dried split peas (2¼ cups), sorted and rinsed

1 teaspoon salt

¼ teaspoon pepper

3 medium carrots, cut crosswise into ¼-inch slices (1½ cups)

2 medium stalks celery, finely chopped (1 cup)

1 small onion, chopped (½ cup)

1 cooked ham bone with meat still attached, 2 pounds ham shanks or 2 pounds smoked pork hocks

Fresh Thyme leaves, if desired

1 SERVING Calories 300; Total Fat 6g (Saturated Fat 2g, Trans Fat 0g); Cholesterol 45mg; Sodium 360mg; Total Carbohydrate 33g (Dietary Fiber 16g); Protein 28g **CARBOHYDRATE CHOICES:** 2

Betty's Kitchen Tip Split peas are a variety of pea grown specifically for drying. Look for them with the dried beans and lentils in your supermarket.

Make Ahead Allow soup to cool; spoon servings into individual microwavable food storage containers. Cover and refrigerate up to 1 week or freeze up to 2 months. To reheat, loosen cover; microwave refrigerated soup on High 2 to 3 minutes, stirring occasionally, or until heated through. Microwave frozen soup 4 to 6 minutes, stirring occasionally and breaking up frozen portions with spoon, until heated through.

1 In 4- to 5-quart slow cooker, mix all ingredients except ham bone. Add ham bone.

2 Cover; cook on Low heat setting 8 to 10 hours or until peas are tender.

3 Remove ham bone from cooker; place on cutting board; let cool until easy enough to handle. Pull meat from bones, using 2 forks; discard skin (if any) and bones. Stir meat into soup. Stir well before serving. Garnish with thyme leaves.

You'll love the two surprises that come with this recipe. First, just how easy it is to make your own freshly baked cauliflower crusts, and second, how yummy pizza can be without a traditional carb-heavy crust!

CARB CHOICES

$\frac{1}{2}$

Mini Cauliflower Pizzas

PREP TIME: 25 Minutes / **START TO FINISH:** 1 Hour 10 Minutes / *4 pizzas*

CRUST

1 bag (12 oz) frozen riced cauliflower
1 egg, beaten
½ cup shredded mozzarella cheese (2 oz)
¼ teaspoon salt
¼ teaspoon pepper
¼ cup shredded Parmesan cheese (1 oz)

TOPPINGS

¼ cup pizza sauce
1 plum (Roma) tomato, thinly sliced
½ cup mozzarella pearls or bocconcini (small fresh mozzarella cheese balls)
2 tablespoons chopped fresh basil leaves

1 Heat oven to 425°F. Line large cookie sheet with cooking parchment paper; spray with cooking spray.

2 Cook cauliflower as directed on bag. Drain cooked cauliflower and spread on paper towels; cool 10 minutes. Place another paper towel over cauliflower and pat top dry.

3 In medium bowl, mix egg, shredded mozzarella cheese, salt and pepper. Stir in cauliflower; mix well.

4 Sprinkle Parmesan cheese in 4 small mounds (1 tablespoon each) on cookie sheet. Place generous ½-cup of cauliflower mixture on top of each mound of Parmesan cheese. Gently shape and press each into a 4½-inch-diameter, ¼-inch-thick patty, smoothing edges.

5 Bake 20 to 25 minutes or until lightly brown. Using pancake turner, gently lift patties from parchment paper and turn over. Top patties evenly with pizza sauce and tomato slices and mozzarella balls. Bake 6 to 8 minutes or until cheese is melted. Top with basil.

1 PIZZA Calories 180; Total Fat 10g (Saturated Fat 3.5g, Trans Fat 0g); Cholesterol 75mg; Sodium 470mg; Total Carbohydrate 8g (Dietary Fiber 2g); Protein 13g **CARBOHYDRATE CHOICES:** ½

Here's a simple snack to prepare when friends drop by or when you're having a family movie night. All the textures and flavors make for an indulgent combination, perfect for when you need "a little something" to nibble on.

Festive Pizza Appetizers

PREP TIME: 15 Minutes / **START TO FINISH:** 15 Minutes / *60 pieces*

1   container (8 oz) dill dip or spinach dip

1   (12-inch) prebaked whole-grain pizza crust (from 2-crust, 16-oz package)

2   cups chopped or thinly sliced fresh vegetables

½   cup finely shredded cheddar cheese (2 oz)

Spread dip over pizza crust to within ½ inch of edge. Sprinkle with vegetables and cheese. Cut into 1½-inch diamond shapes.

1 PIECE Calories 35; Total Fat 1.5g (Saturated Fat 0.5g, Trans Fat 0g); Cholesterol 0mg; Sodium 65mg; Total Carbohydrate 4g (Dietary Fiber 0g); Protein 1g **CARBOHYDRATE CHOICES:** 0

Betty's Kitchen Tip You can vary the veggies and cheese to include your family's favorites, or just use what you have on hand.

For maximum crispness, serve these tasty fries piping hot.

CARB CHOICES

1

Taco Fries

PREP TIME: 10 Minutes / **START TO FINISH:** 40 Minutes / *6 servings*

1¼ lb russet or sweet potatoes (2 or 3 potatoes), peeled

2 tablespoons plus 1 teaspoon Salt-Free Taco Seasoning Mix (page 40)

¼ teaspoon salt

1 Heat oven to 450°F. Spray 15×10×1-inch pan with cooking spray.

2 Cut potatoes in half lengthwise. Cut each half lengthwise into 4 wedges (about 1½ inches on the wide side); place cut side down in pan. Spray potatoes with cooking spray; turn potatoes and spray other side. Sprinkle with taco seasoning mix; toss until potatoes are evenly coated. Arrange potatoes in single layer in pan.

3 Bake uncovered 20 to 25 minutes or until bottoms are crispy. Turn potatoes. Bake about 5 minutes longer or until bottoms are crispy.

1 SERVING Calories 70; Total Fat 0g (Saturated Fat 0g, Trans Fat 0g); Cholesterol 0mg; Sodium 125mg; Total Carbohydrate 14g (Dietary Fiber 1g); Protein 1g **CARBOHYDRATE CHOICES:** 1

Betty's Kitchen Tip If sweet potatoes are used, you can expect a softer texture than if russet potatoes are used.

Crunchy, flavor-packed and just plain fun. These delicious "fries" are seasoned so well they can stand on their own—nothing else required. But if you love to dip, you could try them with one of the dip suggestions below.

CARB CHOICES

$1/2$

Parmesan Carrot Fries

PREP TIME: 10 Minutes / **START TO FINISH:** 30 Minutes / *4 servings (9 carrot fries each)*

3 medium carrots, peeled	2 teaspoons all-purpose flour
2 tablespoons grated Parmesan cheese	1½ teaspoons (from 0.6-oz package) Italian salad dressing mix

1 Heat oven to 425°F. Line cookie sheet with heavy-duty foil; spray with cooking spray.

2 Cut carrots crosswise into about 3-inch lengths. Cut each piece in half lengthwise; cut each piece lengthwise into thirds to make fry-size carrot sticks.

3 In 1 gallon-size resealable food-storage plastic bag, mix Parmesan cheese, flour and salad dressing mix. Add carrots; toss to coat. Spread carrots in single layer on cookie sheet. Sprinkle any remaining cheese mixture over carrots.

4 Bake for 10 minutes. Turn carrots, and bake an additional 7 to 10 minutes or until edges are browned and begin to crisp. Serve immediately.

1 SERVING Calories 40; Total Fat 1g (Saturated Fat 0.5g, Trans Fat 0g); Cholesterol 0mg; Sodium 170mg; Total Carbohydrate 6g (Dietary Fiber 1g); Protein 1g **CARBOHYDRATE CHOICES:** ½

Betty's Kitchen Tip If you like a dip for your fries, try any type of mustard, Tomatillo Salsa (page 44), Smoky Sour Cream and Chive Dip (page 194) or Creamy Herbed Dip (page 142)—but remember to include it in your nutrient calculations for the day.

This colorful and flavorful hummus can be served with your favorite fresh veggies or gluten-free multigrain tortilla chips, for additional carbs.

CARB CHOICES

1/2

Roasted Beet Hummus

PREP TIME: 25 Minutes / **START TO FINISH:** 1 Hour 25 Minutes / *18 servings* (*2 tablespoons each*)

ROASTED VEGETABLES
- ½ lb fresh red beets, peeled and cut in ½-inch wedges
- 2¼ teaspoons olive oil
- ¼ teaspoon salt
- 1 small bulb garlic

HUMMUS
- 1 can (19 oz) chick peas (garbanzo beans), rinsed, drained
- ¼ cup tahini
- 3 tablespoons olive oil
- 2 tablespoons fresh lemon juice
- 2 tablespoons water
- ¾ teaspoon salt

TOPPINGS
- ⅓ cup crumbled feta cheese
- ¼ cup chopped toasted walnuts
- 2 tablespoons finely chopped fresh chives
- 1 teaspoon lemon zest

1 Heat oven to 400°F. Line 15×10×1-inch pan with foil; spray with cooking spray.

2 In small bowl, toss beets with 2 teaspoons of the oil and ¼ teaspoon salt; place in single layer on pan. Remove any loose pieces of papery skin from garlic bulb. Place garlic on small piece of foil (about a 6-inch square), and drizzle with remaining ¼ teaspoon olive oil; pull up sides of foil around garlic, twist corners together and place on pan with beets.

3 Bake 35 to 40 minutes or until beets are tender and garlic is soft. Let cool 20 minutes.

4 Into food processor, gently squeeze 6 cloves of the roasted garlic; add beets and all hummus ingredients. Cover; process 2 to 3 minutes, scraping sides occasionally, until smooth.

5 Spoon hummus into serving bowl; sprinkle with toppings.

1 SERVING Calories 100; Total Fat 7g (Saturated Fat 1g, Trans Fat 0g); Cholesterol 0mg; Sodium 220mg; Total Carbohydrate 7g (Dietary Fiber 2g); Protein 3g **CARBOHYDRATE CHOICES:** ½

Betty's Kitchen Tip Roasting garlic results in a richer, more mellow flavor than fresh garlic. You can refrigerate the remaining cloves in a resealable food-storage plastic bag up to 3 days or freeze up to 1 month, to add to other recipes.

Betty's Kitchen Tip The beautiful, deep red juice of beets can stain cutting boards and some work surfaces if left too long. Simply rinse juice-covered areas with cool water immediately after cutting to avoid stains.

Whether spooned over grilled vegetables or used as a spread for wraps or a dip for crudités, this fresh, citrusy herbal dip perks up any meal or snack.

Creamy Herbed Dip

PREP TIME: 10 Minutes / **START TO FINISH:** 10 Minutes / *12 servings* (*about 1½ tablespoons each*)

1⅓ cups plain low-fat Greek yogurt

¼ cup finely chopped fresh chives

2 tablespoons finely chopped fresh parsley

2 tablespoons chopped fresh basil leaves

1 teaspoon fresh lemon juice

¼ teaspoon salt

1 clove garlic, finely chopped

In medium bowl, mix all ingredients. Cover; refrigerate until you're ready to serve, up to 4 days. Stir before serving.

1 SERVING Calories 20; Total Fat 0.5g (Saturated Fat 0g, Trans Fat 0g); Cholesterol 0mg; Sodium 60mg; Total Carbohydrate 1g (Dietary Fiber 0g); Protein 3g **CARBOHYDRATE CHOICES:** 0

Make It Your Own Experiment with other herbs such as 1 tablespoon chopped fresh tarragon instead of the basil, or green onion instead of chives.

Sure to be popular at any gathering, serve these tasty little bites on decorative toothpicks, so guests can grab and eat them easily.

CARB CHOICES

0

Turkey-Parmesan Cheese Balls

PREP TIME: 20 Minutes / **START TO FINISH:** 40 Minutes / *48 appetizer balls*

- 2 cups shredded Italian cheese blend (8 oz)
- 1½ cups Original Bisquick™ mix
- ½ lb bulk mild Italian or hot turkey sausage
- ½ cup Italian-style panko crispy bread crumbs
- ½ cup milk
- ¼ cup butter, melted
- 1 tablespoon Italian seasoning
- 1 teaspoon garlic powder
- ½ cup grated Parmesan cheese
- 1 cup marinara sauce, warmed

1 Heat oven to 350°F. Line bottom and sides of 15×10×1-inch pan with foil. Generously spray with cooking spray.

2 In large bowl, stir together all ingredients except Parmesan cheese and marinara sauce, using hands or spoon. Shape mixture into 48 (1-inch) balls. Place Parmesan cheese in small bowl. Roll balls in Parmesan cheese, pressing to adhere. Place in pan.

3 Bake 18 to 23 minutes or until brown, cooked through in center and instant-read meat thermometer reads 165°F. Immediately remove from pan. Serve warm with sauce.

1 APPETIZER BALL Calories 60; Total Fat 3.5g (Saturated Fat 2g, Trans Fat 0g); Cholesterol 10mg; Sodium 160mg; Total Carbohydrate 4g (Dietary Fiber 0g); Protein 3g **CARBOHYDRATE CHOICES:** 0

Betty's Kitchen Tip Lining the pan with foil and spraying it generously with cooking spray will ensure the delicious Parmesan cheese coating won't stick to the pan.

These little balls are chock-full of yummy ingredients. They store and travel well, making them a good choice to carry as a snack in your purse or bag. If you like, keep the sesame seeds or nuts out of the balls to roll them in, instead.

CARB CHOICES

1

Energy Balls 3 Ways

PREP TIME: 20 Minutes / **START TO FINISH:** 50 Minutes / *16 servings (2 balls each)*

CHOCOLATE–PEANUT BUTTER ENERGY BALLS

1¼ cups old-fashioned oats

1 cup creamy peanut butter

¼ cup miniature semisweet chocolate chips

2 tablespoons vanilla protein powder

1 tablespoon chia seed

3 tablespoons honey

ALMOND BUTTER–CRANBERRY ENERGY BALLS

1¼ cups old-fashioned oats

1 cup almond butter

1 tablespoon flax seed

3 tablespoons honey

⅛ teaspoon salt

½ cup sweetened dried cranberries, chopped

¼ cup toasted almonds, chopped

SPICY CASHEW-SESAME ENERGY BALLS

1 jar (12 oz) cashew butter (about 1¼ cups)

1¼ cups old-fashioned oats

1 tablespoon vanilla protein powder

1 tablespoon toasted sesame seed

⅛ teaspoon salt

¼ teaspoon ground red pepper (cayenne)

3 tablespoons honey

1 Line large cookie sheet with cooking parchment paper.

2 Select the type of energy ball to prepare. In medium bowl, stir together all ingredients until well mixed. Shape into 32 (1-inch) balls. Place on cookie sheet.

3 Cover; refrigerate 30 minutes.

1 SERVING (Chocolate–Peanut Butter Balls) Calories 170; Total Fat 10g (Saturated Fat 2.5g, Trans Fat 0g); Cholesterol 0mg; Sodium 75mg; Total Carbohydrate 13g (Dietary Fiber 2g); Protein 6g **CARBOHYDRATE CHOICES:** 1

Betty's Kitchen Tip We love the depth of flavor these balls have when the oats are toasted before being mixed with the other ingredients: Spread oats in 15×10×1-inch pan. Bake at 350°F for 5 to 6 minutes or until golden brown.

Betty's Kitchen Tip Natural nut butters such as almond butter and cashew butter often separate upon standing, so they require a lot of stirring to mix the oil back in before using. If you are using an entire jar of one of these butters, you can save some time by dumping it into the bowl (without mixing first) along with the other ingredients. Mix with an electric mixer on low speed for 2 to 3 minutes and continue as directed. You may find yourself with a few bonus energy balls when you mix them this way.

Betty's Kitchen Tip You can purchase sesame seed toasted, which makes those balls come together faster, or you can toast your own: Place sesame seed in 8-inch skillet and cook over medium heat 2 to 3 minutes, stirring frequently, or until golden brown. Immediately remove from pan to prevent additional browning.

Betty's Kitchen Tip Store the energy balls in an airtight container in the refrigerator up to 2 weeks or in the freezer up to 2 months.

If your apples are very thinly sliced, and golden brown when you remove them from the oven, they will crisp as they cool.

CARB CHOICES

3

Easy Baked Apple Chips

PREP TIME: 15 Minutes / **START TO FINISH:** 4 Hours / *4 servings*

2 large Granny Smith apples

½ cup organic sugar

1 teaspoon ground cinnamon

1 SERVING Calories 170; Total Fat 0g (Saturated Fat 0g, Trans Fat 0g); Cholesterol 0mg; Sodium 0mg; Total Carbohydrate 41g (Dietary Fiber 3g); Protein 0g **CARBOHYDRATE CHOICES:** 3

1 Heat oven to 225°F. Line two 18×13-inch half-sheet pans with cooking parchment paper; spray with cooking spray. Using a mandoline slicer on the thinnest setting, use firm pressure to slice apples into rounds, starting from bottom end. Remove the seeds from slices as necessary.

2 In small bowl, mix sugar and cinnamon. On work surface, sprinkle both sides of apple slices with cinnamon mixture; place in single layer on pans.

3 Bake about 1 hour, rotating pans halfway through, or until apples are golden brown. Cool pan on cooling rack 10 to 15 minutes before serving.

Betty's Kitchen Tip Once apples are baked, they will start to pick up moisture and lose some of their crispiness. They are best eaten shortly after making.

Betty's Kitchen Tip The thinner the apple slices, the crisper they will get. Mandoline slicers are best to ensure your apples are sliced thin enough to get crisp.

This savory snack is great for tailgating on game day and for everyday parties. The crispy textures make it fun to nibble.

CARB CHOICES

1

Spicy White Cheddar Mix

PREP TIME: 10 Minutes / **START TO FINISH:** 50 Minutes / *20 servings (½ cup each)*

- 4 cups bite-size squares oven-toasted corn cereal
- 2 cups bite-size squares 100% whole-grain wheat cereal
- 2 cups bite-size white cheddar cheese crackers
- 1 cup mini unsalted pretzel twists
- 1 cup mixed nuts
- ¼ cup butter
- 3 tablespoons red pepper sauce

1 SERVING Calories 140; Total Fat 7g (Saturated Fat 2g, Trans Fat 0g); Cholesterol 5mg; Sodium 240mg; Total Carbohydrate 16g (Dietary Fiber 1g); Protein 2g **CARBOHYDRATE CHOICES:** 1

Microwave Spicy White Cheddar Mix

In large microwavable bowl, mix cereals, crackers, pretzels and nuts; set aside. In small microwavable bowl, microwave butter uncovered on High 30 seconds or until melted. Stir in pepper sauce. Pour over cereal mixture in bowl; stir until evenly coated. Microwave uncovered on High 4 to 5 minutes, stirring thoroughly after every minute, or until evenly toasted. Spread on waxed paper to cool completely, about 20 minutes.

1 Heat oven to 325°F.

2 In large bowl, mix cereals, crackers, pretzels and nuts; set aside. In 1-quart saucepan, heat butter and pepper sauce over medium-low heat until butter is melted. Pour over cereal mixture in bowl; stir until evenly coated. Spread in ungreased 15×10×1-inch pan.

3 Bake 15 to 20 minutes, carefully stirring twice, or until mixture is toasted. Spread on waxed paper to cool completely, about 20 minutes. To serve, transfer mixture to large serving bowl. Store at room temperature in covered container.

Look for the dried berries near the other dried fruits like raisins or prunes, or near the nuts or bulk foods in your grocery store.

CARB CHOICES

1

Dark Chocolate Berry Trail Mix

PREP TIME: 5 Minutes / **START TO FINISH:** 5 Minutes / *4 servings (½ cup each)*

1 cup O-shaped honey-nut cereal

½ cup freeze-dried strawberries

¼ cup freeze-dried raspberries

2 tablespoons vegan extra-dark bittersweet (at least 63% cacao) chocolate chips

2 tablespoons roasted, salted whole almonds

In medium bowl, mix all ingredients; gently stir to combine. Store tightly covered at room temperature.

1 SERVING Calories 120; Total Fat 5g (Saturated Fat 1g, Trans Fat 0g); Cholesterol 0mg; Sodium 85mg; Total Carbohydrate 16g (Dietary Fiber 3g); Protein 2g **CARBOHYDRATE CHOICES:** 1

Fluffer-nutter flavors inspired this ooey-gooey treat. For best eating, we recommend serving this snack mix the same day you make it.

CARB CHOICES
1

Marshmallow Peanut Butter Snack Mix

PREP TIME: 15 Minutes / **START TO FINISH:** 45 Minutes / *14 servings (½ cup each)*

4 cups bite-size squares peanut butter oven-toasted corn cereal

1 cup marshmallow creme (from 7-oz jar)

¼ cup peanut butter chips

1 tablespoon butter

¾ cups mini peanut butter sandwich cookies

¾ cups miniature vegan marshmallows

½ cup dry-roasted peanuts

1 Line 15×10×1-inch pan with waxed paper. Spray large bowl with cooking spray; add cereal to bowl.

2 In medium microwavable bowl, microwave marshmallow creme, peanut butter chips and butter uncovered on High about 30 seconds, stirring after 15 seconds, or until mixture is melted and can be stirred smooth.

3 Pour over cereal, stirring well. Microwave mixture uncovered on High 1 to 2 minutes, stirring after every minute until mixture is well coated. Spread on pan; cool 10 minutes. Break into bite-size clusters; cool completely.

4 In large serving bowl, stir together cereal clusters, cookies, marshmallows and peanuts.

1 SERVING Calories 130; Total Fat 5g (Saturated Fat 1.5g, Trans Fat 0g); Cholesterol 0mg; Sodium 130mg; Total Carbohydrate 18g (Dietary Fiber 1g); Protein 2g **CARBOHYDRATE CHOICES:** 1

Betty's Kitchen Tip Spraying your spoon or spatula with cooking spray helps keep the marshmallow mixture from clinging to it when you stir the cereal mixture.

Carrot-Mango Smoothie Poppers and Blueberry-Grape
and Lime Green Smoothie Poppers (pages 158–159)

Look for carrot juice in the refrigerated case of the produce section of your grocery store. Or if you have a juicer, you can make your own. If you like, you can cut these little snacks with 1-inch cookie cutters. You'll get about 18, plus scraps.

CARB CHOICES

0

Carrot-Mango Smoothie Poppers

PREP TIME: 10 Minutes / **START TO FINISH:** 4 Hours 10 Minutes / *24 servings*

2 envelopes unflavored gelatin

¼ cup chilled carrot juice

½ cup chopped ripe mango

2 containers (6 oz each) French vanilla or mango low-fat yogurt

¾ cup apple juice, heated to boiling

1 Lightly spray 9×5-inch loaf pan with cooking spray; blot with paper towel. Set aside.

2 In large bowl, sprinkle gelatin on cold carrot juice to soften; let stand 1 minute. Meanwhile, in blender, place mango and yogurt. Cover; blend on high speed until smooth.

3 Add hot apple juice to gelatin mixture; stir about 2 minutes or until gelatin is dissolved. Stir in yogurt mixture. Pour into loaf pan. Cover; refrigerate until firm, about 4 hours.

4 Cut into cubes and serve, or cover and refrigerate up to 2 days before serving.

1 SERVING Calories 25; Total Fat 0g (Saturated Fat 0g, Trans Fat 0g); Cholesterol 0mg; Sodium 10mg; Total Carbohydrate 4g (Dietary Fiber 0g); Protein 1g **CARBOHYDRATE CHOICES:** 0

Concord grape juice, found in the juice aisle of your grocery store, gives this fun snack a lot of flavor and color.

CARB CHOICES
1/2

Blueberry-Grape Smoothie Poppers

PREP TIME: 10 Minutes / **START TO FINISH:** 4 Hours 10 Minutes / *24 servings*

2 envelopes unflavored gelatin

½ cup chilled Concord grape juice

½ cup fresh blueberries

2 containers (6 oz each) French vanilla low-fat yogurt

¾ cup Concord grape juice, heated to boiling

1 Lightly spray 9×5-inch loaf pan with cooking spray; blot with paper towel. Set aside.

2 In large bowl, sprinkle gelatin on cold grape juice to soften; let stand 1 minute. Meanwhile, in blender, place blueberries and yogurt. Cover; blend on high speed until smooth.

3 Add hot grape juice to gelatin mixture; stir about 2 minutes or until gelatin is dissolved. Stir in yogurt mixture. Pour into loaf pan. Cover; refrigerate until firm, about 4 hours.

4 Cut into cubes and serve, or cover and refrigerate up to 2 days before serving.

1 SERVING Calories 25; Total Fat 0g (Saturated Fat 0g, Trans Fat 0g); Cholesterol 0mg; Sodium 10mg; Total Carbohydrate 5g (Dietary Fiber 0g); Protein 1g **CARBOHYDRATE CHOICES:** ½

You can use small (about 1-inch) cookie cutters to give the poppers festive shapes. Deeper ones will more easily cut through the thick frozen mixture. You will get about 18 servings if you cut them this way.

CARB CHOICES

0

Lime Green Smoothie Poppers

PREP TIME: 10 Minutes / **START TO FINISH:** 4 Hours 10 Minutes / *24 servings*

2 envelopes unflavored gelatin

½ cup chilled apple juice

½ cup packed fresh baby spinach leaves

2 containers (6 oz each) Key lime low-fat yogurt

¾ cup apple juice, heated to boiling

1 Lightly spray 9×5-inch loaf pan with cooking spray; blot with paper towel. Set aside.

2 In large bowl, sprinkle gelatin on cold apple juice to soften; let stand 1 minute. Meanwhile, in blender, place spinach and yogurt. Cover; blend on high speed until smooth.

3 Add hot apple juice to gelatin mixture; stir about 2 minutes or until gelatin is dissolved. Stir in yogurt mixture. Pour into loaf pan. Cover; refrigerate until firm, about 4 hours.

4 Cut into cubes and serve, or cover and refrigerate up to 2 days before serving.

1 SERVING Calories 15; Total Fat 0g (Saturated Fat 0g, Trans Fat 0g); Cholesterol 0mg; Sodium 10mg; Total Carbohydrate 3g (Dietary Fiber 0g); Protein 1g **CARBOHYDRATE CHOICES:** 0

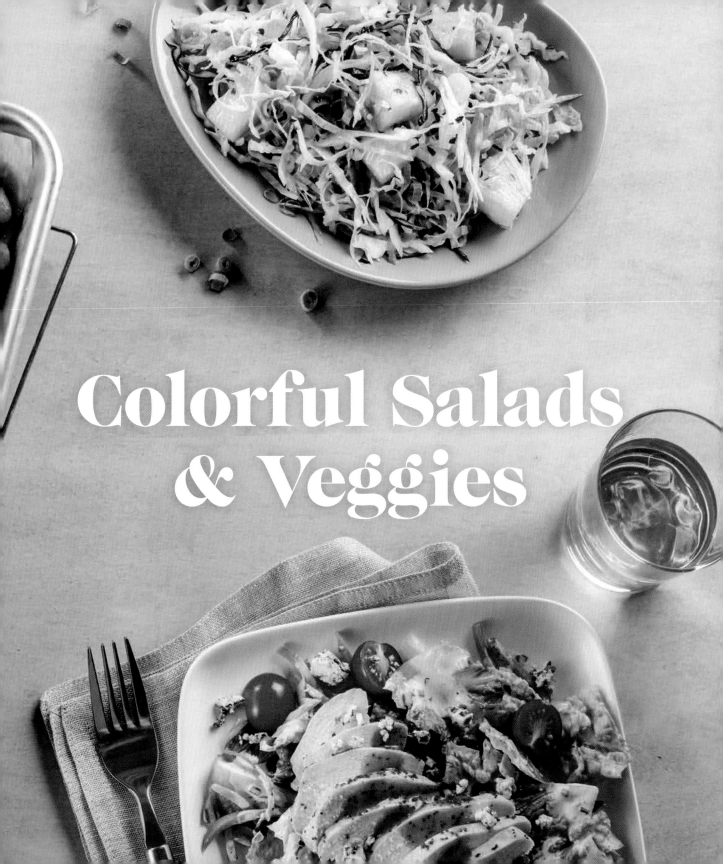

Colorful Salads & Veggies

A light, fresh-tasting dressing makes this salad truly unique. If you like, sprinkle the salad with a little pepper when tossing it together.

CARB CHOICES

1

Thai-Style Chopped Salad

PREP TIME: 25 Minutes / **START TO FINISH:** 25 Minutes / *4 servings (1½ cups each)*

3 cups coarsely chopped bok choy leaves and stems

1 cup diced fresh mango

½ cup shredded carrot (about 1 medium)

½ medium red bell pepper, cut into 1×¼-inch strips (½ cup)

½ cup fresh snow peas, cut diagonally into 1-inch pieces

3 medium green onions, sliced (about 3 tablespoons)

2 tablespoons chopped fresh cilantro leaves

Peanut Coriander Dressing (page 48)

¼ teaspoon salt

2 tablespoons sliced almonds, toasted

Pepper, if desired

1 In large bowl, gently toss together all ingredients except the dressing, salt, pepper and sliced almonds.

2 In small bowl, stir together dressing and salt. Drizzle dressing over salad; toss gently to coat. Sprinkle with almonds and pepper. Serve immediately.

1 SERVING Calories 150; Total Fat 7g (Saturated Fat 2.5g, Trans Fat 0g); Cholesterol 0mg; Sodium 360mg; Total Carbohydrate 16g (Dietary Fiber 3g); Protein 5g **CARBOHYDRATE CHOICES: 1**

Betty's Kitchen Tip Bok choy is a type of Chinese cabbage. Both the stems and the mild-flavored leaves are edible, and add crunch and color to this pretty salad. It grows in sandy soil, so be sure to rinse the stalks well to remove the sand that can hide between them.

What is it about Buffalo chicken that makes it seem so indulgent? Whether it's the spicy sauce or the blue cheese, you'll love this diabetes-friendly salad version.

CARB CHOICES

1

Buffalo Chicken Salad

PREP TIME: 20 Minutes / **START TO FINISH:** 45 Minutes / *4 servings*

CHICKEN

- 1 teaspoon butter
- ¼ cup Buffalo wing sauce
- 1 teaspoon celery seed
- 2 boneless skinless chicken breasts (about ¾ lb total)

DRESSING

- ½ cup plain nonfat Greek yogurt
- 2 tablespoons light mayonnaise
- 1 tablespoon fresh lemon juice
- 1 tablespoon water
- 1 teaspoon gluten-free reduced-sodium Worcestershire sauce

- ½ teaspoon pepper
- ¼ teaspoon sugar
- 1 clove garlic, finely chopped
- 2 tablespoons finely chopped fresh chives
- 2 tablespoons finely chopped parsley

SALAD

- 1 bag (10 oz) chopped hearts of romaine lettuce (about 6 cups)
- 1 cup shredded carrot (about 1 medium)
- 1½ cups cherry tomatoes, cut in half
- 2 tablespoons crumbled blue cheese

1 Heat oven to 425°F. Line cookie sheet with foil and spray with cooking spray.

2 In medium microwavable bowl, place butter. Microwave uncovered on High 30 to 45 seconds or until melted. Add Buffalo wing sauce and celery seed; stir to mix. Set aside 2 tablespoons sauce mixture in small bowl. Add chicken breasts to remaining sauce mixture; toss to coat.

3 Transfer chicken to cookie sheet. Bake 15 to 20 minutes or until juice of chicken is clear when center of thickest part is cut and instant-read meat thermometer reads 165°F.

4 Meanwhile, in large bowl, beat all dressing ingredients except chives and parsley.

5 Transfer chicken breasts to cutting board; slice thin. To serve, stir chives and parsley into dressing. Toss lettuce and carrot in dressing. Divide mixture among 4 plates. Top with tomatoes. Divide chicken evenly over salads. Drizzle reserved sauce mixture over chicken and top with blue cheese.

1 SERVING Calories 230; Total Fat 9g (Saturated Fat 3g, Trans Fat 0g); Cholesterol 60mg; Sodium 410mg; Total Carbohydrate 12g (Dietary Fiber 3g); Protein 25g **CARBOHYDRATE CHOICES: 1**

Betty's Kitchen Tip If you don't have celery seed on hand, you can leave it out of the sauce and add some chopped fresh celery to the salad instead.

Betty's Kitchen Tip You can make the salad dressing up to 3 days in advance; cover and refrigerate it until you're ready to put together the salad. It will make getting the salad on the table that much faster—and the flavors mix and mingle more when they get to hang out together longer!

Quinoa is a tiny pearl-shaped, ivory-colored grain that expands to three times its size when cooked. It adapts well to just about any flavors you put with it. If you like, serve this salad on a bed of lettuce.

CARB CHOICES

2½

Quinoa and Vegetable Salad

PREP TIME: 10 Minutes / **START TO FINISH:** 1 Hour 40 Minutes / *6 servings (about 1½ cups each)*

1 cup uncooked quinoa, rinsed, well drained

2 tablespoons chopped fresh basil leaves

2 tablespoons fresh lemon juice

2 tablespoons olive oil

1 can (15 oz) whole kernel sweet corn, drained

1 can (15 oz) chick peas (garbanzo beans), rinsed, drained

1 can (14.5 oz) diced tomatoes, drained

1 cup chopped red bell pepper

⅓ cup quartered pitted black or kalamata olives

½ cup crumbled gluten-free feta cheese (2 oz)

1 Cook quinoa as directed on package; drain. Cool completely, about 30 minutes.

2 Meanwhile, in small nonmetal bowl, add basil, lemon juice and oil; mix well.

3 In large bowl, toss quinoa, corn, chick peas, tomatoes, bell pepper and olives. Pour lemon juice mixture over quinoa mixture; toss gently to coat. Serve immediately, or refrigerate 1 to 2 hours before serving. Just before serving, sprinkle with cheese.

1 SERVING Calories 300; Total Fat 11g (Saturated Fat 2.5g, Trans Fat 0g); Cholesterol 10mg; Sodium 440mg; Total Carbohydrate 40g (Dietary Fiber 8g); Protein 10g **CARBOHYDRATE CHOICES:** 2½

"Tuh-BOO-lee" is a great choice to bring to a potluck, as the ingredients stand up well without getting soggy. It makes a terrific side dish for any grilled or broiled chicken, meat or fish, a flavorful base to a bowl meal or a vegetarian filling for pita pockets.

CARB CHOICES

1

Barley, Cauliflower and Red Lentil "Tabbouleh"

PREP TIME: 10 Minutes / **START TO FINISH:** 2 Hours 10 Minutes / *15 servings (½ cup each)*

SALAD

- ½ cup uncooked hulled barley
- 2¼ cups water
- 1 cup dried red lentils, sorted, rinsed
- 2 cups 1-inch fresh cauliflower florets, separated into mini florets (about ¼ inch)
- 1 cup chopped fresh parsley
- 1 cup crumbled feta cheese (4 oz)
- ½ cup chopped fresh mint leaves
- 1 jar (12 oz) roasted red bell peppers, drained, patted dry and chopped

DRESSING

- 3 tablespoons olive oil
- 3 tablespoons fresh lemon juice
- 1¼ teaspoons Greek seasoning or salt

1 In 2-quart saucepan, heat barley and water to boiling; reduce heat. Cover; simmer 40 minutes. Add lentils; cook 10 to 15 minutes longer or until barley is chewy but tender and lentils are just tender. (Do not overcook or lentils will lose their shape and become mushy.) Let stand 5 minutes or until liquid is absorbed. Place in fine-mesh strainer; rinse with cold water. Drain well.

2 In medium bowl, place barley, lentils and remaining salad ingredients. In tightly covered container, shake dressing ingredients. Pour over salad mixture; gently toss to combine. Cover; refrigerate at least 1 hour to blend flavors. Cover and refrigerate any remaining salad up to 4 days.

1 SERVING Calories 120; Total Fat 4.5g (Saturated Fat 1.5g, Trans Fat 0g); Cholesterol 5mg; Sodium 380mg; Total Carbohydrate 15g (Dietary Fiber 4g); Protein 5g **CARBOHYDRATE CHOICES:** 1

Start with some Make-Ahead Cilantro-Lime Barley (page 34) and this salad is fork ready in 15 minutes. We love the combination of fruit and vegetables with the black beans and barley—it's so fresh!

CARB CHOICES 1½

Strawberry Black Bean Barley Salad

PREP TIME: 15 Minutes / **START TO FINISH:** 1 Hour 15 Minutes / *8 servings (½ cup each)*

SALAD

1⅔ cups Make-Ahead Cilantro-Lime Barley (page 34)

1 cup quartered hulled fresh strawberries

1 can (15 oz) reduced-sodium black beans, rinsed, drained

3 medium green onions, thinly sliced (about 3 tablespoons)

½ medium avocado, pitted, peeled and diced

CITRUS VINAIGRETTE

2 teaspoons orange zest

¼ cup fresh orange juice

2 tablespoons finely chopped red onion

1 tablespoon plus 1 teaspoon olive oil

1 tablespoon chopped fresh chives

¼ plus ⅛ teaspoon salt

Dash pepper

Additional chopped fresh chives, if desired

1 In medium bowl, stir together all salad ingredients except avocado.

2 In jar, place all vinaigrette ingredients; cover and shake well. Pour vinaigrette over salad; toss to coat. Gently stir in avocado. Cover; refrigerate about 1 hour or until flavors are blended. Sprinkle with additional chives.

1 SERVING Calories 150; Total Fat 4g (Saturated Fat 0.5g, Trans Fat 0g); Cholesterol 0mg; Sodium 125mg; Total Carbohydrate 23g (Dietary Fiber 7g); Protein 5g **CARBOHYDRATE CHOICES:** 1½

Curry powder, lime and jalapeño give this black bean salad a Caribbean twist. It would be amazing with grilled chicken or pork chops prepared with Strawberry Barbecue Sauce (page 53).

CARB CHOICES

1

Mango-Black Bean Salad

PREP TIME: 25 Minutes / **START TO FINISH:** 25 Minutes / *8 servings (½ cup each)*

- 1 can (15 oz) black beans, rinsed, drained
- 1 cup diced fresh mango
- ½ cup chopped red bell pepper
- ¼ cup finely chopped red onion
- ¼ cup chopped fresh cilantro
- 3 tablespoons fresh lime juice
- 2 tablespoons olive oil
- 1 tablespoon seeded finely chopped jalapeño chile
- 1 teaspoon curry powder
- ½ teaspoon salt

In medium bowl, mix all ingredients until well coated.

1 SERVING Calories 110; Total Fat 4g (Saturated Fat 0.5g, Trans Fat 0g); Cholesterol 0mg; Sodium 300mg; Total Carbohydrate 15g (Dietary Fiber 5g); Protein 3g **CARBOHYDRATE CHOICES:** 1

Betty's Kitchen Tip When using raw red onions, rinsing the chopped onions under cold water helps take the "bite" out of the otherwise strong flavor.

Betty's Kitchen Tip To peel a mango, first stand the fruit on its less-pointy end and use a knife to cut straight down on either side, avoiding the large seed in the middle. Cut a crosshatch pattern into the flesh of each half, then turn inside out to make diced mango.

Jicama is a crunchy root vegetable with a sweet, nutty flavor that's popular in Mexican cuisine. Its pretty ivory color does not become discolored, which makes it a natural choice to use in salads like this one.

CARB CHOICES 1

Spicy Jicama and Orange Salad

PREP TIME: 30 Minutes / **START TO FINISH:** 1 Hour / *8 servings (1 cup each)*

DRESSING

- 2 tablespoons plain low-fat yogurt
- 1 tablespoon white wine vinegar
- 1 tablespoon agave nectar
- 1½ teaspoons Dijon mustard
- ¾ teaspoon chili garlic paste
- ¼ teaspoon ground cumin
- ⅛ teaspoon salt
- ⅛ teaspoon ground coriander
- ⅛ teaspoon pepper

SALAD

- ½ lb jicama, peeled, cut into julienne pieces (3×¼×¼ inch)
- ½ English (hothouse) cucumber, cut into julienne pieces (3×¼×¼ inch; about 1 cup)
- 4 oranges, peeled, sectioned
- ½ cup chopped fresh cilantro

1 In large bowl, beat all dressing ingredients with whisk.

2 Add jicama, cucumber and oranges; toss to coat. Let stand at room temperature about 30 minutes to blend flavors.

3 Before serving, top with cilantro.

1 SERVING Calories 60; Total Fat 0g (Saturated Fat 0g, Trans Fat 0g); Cholesterol 0mg; Sodium 75mg; Total Carbohydrate 13g (Dietary Fiber 3g); Protein 1g **CARBOHYDRATE CHOICES:** 1

Betty's Kitchen Tip Chili garlic paste is made from red chiles, fermented beans and garlic. It's available in most supermarkets in the Asian ingredients section.

This tropical take on coleslaw will perk up any meal whether it's served alongside burgers or chicken or on top of pulled pork sandwiches.

CARB CHOICES
$\frac{1}{2}$

Easy Pineapple Slaw

PREP TIME: 10 Minutes / **START TO FINISH:** 10 Minutes / *6 servings (about ¾ cup each)*

- 4 cups coleslaw mix (from a 14-oz bag)
- ¾ cup diced fresh pineapple
- ¼ cup sliced green onions (4 medium)

- 3 tablespoons fresh lime juice
- 1 tablespoon honey
- 1 teaspoon canola oil
- ¼ teaspoon salt
- ¼ teaspoon crushed red pepper flakes

In medium bowl, toss all ingredients until evenly coated.

1 SERVING Calories 50; Total Fat 1g (Saturated Fat 0g, Trans Fat 0g); Cholesterol 0mg; Sodium 110mg; Total Carbohydrate 9g (Dietary Fiber 1g); Protein 1g **CARBOHYDRATE CHOICES:** ½

Crisp red apples such as Gala or Braeburn are great choices for this recipe.

Kale and Apple Slaw

PREP TIME: 20 Minutes / **START TO FINISH:** 1 Hour 20 Minutes / *6 servings (about 1 cup each)*

SALAD

- 1 bunch (8 oz) kale, stems removed, cut into very thin strips (about 6 cups)
- 1 medium crisp apple, cut into julienne pieces (about 1½ cups)
- ½ medium red onion, sliced

DRESSING

- 3 tablespoons red wine vinegar
- 3 tablespoons fresh lime juice
- 2 tablespoons honey
- 1 tablespoon olive oil
- 2 teaspoons gluten-free Worcestershire sauce
- ½ teaspoon pepper

1 In large bowl, toss salad ingredients to mix.

2 In small bowl, mix dressing ingredients until well blended. Pour dressing over salad; toss to thoroughly coat. Let stand at room temperature 1 hour to blend flavors, stirring occasionally. Cover; refrigerate until serving time.

1 SERVING Calories 90; Total Fat 2.5g (Saturated Fat 0g, Trans Fat 0g); Cholesterol 0mg; Sodium 35mg; Total Carbohydrate 16g (Dietary Fiber 1g); Protein 1g **CARBOHYDRATE CHOICES:** 1

Betty's Kitchen Tip To cut the apple into julienne (matchstick-size) pieces, core the apple and cut into ¼-inch-thick slices. Stack the slices on top of each other and cut into ¼-inch-wide sticks.

ADDING FLAVOR WITHOUT SALT

If you're looking to watch or reduce the amount of salt you eat, here are some terrific tips we use in the Betty Crocker Kitchens to keep sodium (as salt is known on food labels) in check. Salt—chemically, sodium chloride—plays many important roles in food. Salt may be added to foods not only for its own flavor, but also for color and texture, to preserve food and to intensify or balance other flavors. Sodium is present naturally in almost all foods. So how is it possible to limit the sodium in food?

Boost Flavor While Lowering Sodium

- **Substitute Lower-Sodium Products** where possible, such as broths, canned beans and tomatoes, and condiments like ketchup or soy sauce. Make your own seasoning blends such as Salt-Free Taco Seasoning Mix (page 40) and salad dressings, where you can control the amount of salt you add.

- **Make Your Own** meals so you can control how much salt is added.

- **Season the Parts** rather than seasoning the finished dish. Try splitting a reduced amount of salt between the different parts. For example, season the chicken in a one-pot meal with a little before cooking, then season the veggies before you add them. You can trick your tastebuds into thinking there is more salt in the dish than there is!

- **Marinate to Infuse Flavor** using low- or no-sodium marinades or rubs on meats or veggies to add flavor to every bite.

- **Sprinkle, Squeeze or Drizzle** low- or no-sodium ingredients over finished dishes for a burst of flavor.

FLAVOR-PACKED LOW- OR NO-SODIUM INGREDIENTS

Use these ingredients to flavor your food without a lot of added sodium.

Chiles	Add dried or fresh chiles to marinades or rubs. Add dried chiles to dishes while they cook; use fresh chiles as garnish for finished dishes.
Citrus Juice	Add to marinades; squeeze over cooked veggies, grains, pasta or fruit.
Citrus Zest	Add to marinades; toss with cooked grains, pasta or veggies; add to salads.
Flavored Vinegars	Add to marinades; use as salad dressing by itself or with a small amount of a healthy oil; sprinkle over veggies or fruit.
Fruit Juice	Add a splash to marinades or salad dressings, or to sparkling water for a hint of fresh flavor. Fruit juices do contain sugar, so use sparingly.
Garlic	Add raw or roasted to marinades or rubs; sprinkle over meat or chicken before cooking; add to meat, potato, rice or veggie dishes as they cook; add to salad dressings.
Green Onions or Chives	Add to marinades or salad dressings; add to meat, potato, rice or vegetable dishes; sprinkle over cooked dishes for color as well as flavor.
Herbs	Add dried herbs to marinades or dishes while they cook; add fresh herbs during cooking or use to garnish cooked dish. Experiment with different herbs and herb combinations.
Horseradish	Spread over roasts before cooking; add to yogurt for dipping sauce; add to marinades. Check labels for low-sodium products.
Onions or Shallots	Add, or bump up the amount used in cooked dishes, salads and veggies.
Salsa	Use to top cooked eggs, Mexican-style dishes and cooked chicken, fish or meat.
Spices	Sprinkle over hot cereals or grains for breakfast, or fruit anytime.

This fresh take on the classic is a delicious and refreshing side for summer grilling, picnics and potlucks.

CARB CHOICES

0

Creamy Cucumber Salad

PREP TIME: 15 Minutes / **START TO FINISH:** 15 Minutes / *6 servings*

½ cup sour cream

1 tablespoon white wine vinegar

2 teaspoons chopped fresh dill weed

½ teaspoon salt

¼ teaspoon pepper

1 large English (hothouse) cucumber, cut in half lengthwise, then cut crosswise into ¼-inch slices (about 3½ cups)

¼ cup thinly sliced red onion

Fresh dill sprig, if desired

1 In large bowl, beat sour cream, white wine vinegar, dill weed, salt and pepper with whisk.

2 Just before serving, add cucumber and red onion to sour cream mixture, tossing to coat. Garnish with dill sprig. Serve immediately.

1 SERVING Calories 50; Total Fat 4g (Saturated Fat 2g, Trans Fat 0g); Cholesterol 10mg; Sodium 210mg; Total Carbohydrate 3g (Dietary Fiber 0g); Protein 0g **CARBOHYDRATE CHOICES:** 0

Betty's Kitchen Tip Cucumbers will start to give up water after standing, so this salad is best assembled just before serving. If you slice the cucumber ahead of time, drain off any liquid before you assemble the salad.

To quickly slice the cauliflower, run the florets through your food processor with the slicer blade attached.

CARB CHOICES

1

Apple-Cauliflower Salad

PREP TIME: 30 Minutes / **START TO FINISH:** 1 Hour / *12 servings (¾ cup each)*

3 tablespoons fresh lemon juice

1 tablespoon vegan Dijon mustard

¾ teaspoon salt

2 tablespoons olive oil

1 tablespoon fresh thyme leaves, chopped

1 medium head cauliflower (2 lb), broken into florets, thinly sliced (about 6 cups)

2 cups shredded green cabbage

½ cup sliced red onion

1 green apple, cut into julienne pieces

½ cup chopped walnuts, toasted

½ cup unsweetened dried cranberries

1 In large bowl, beat lemon juice, mustard and salt with whisk. Slowly beat in olive oil; stir in thyme.

2 Add cauliflower, cabbage, red onion and apple; toss to coat. Stir in walnuts and cranberries; toss. Cover; refrigerate 30 minutes before serving.

1 SERVING Calories 100; Total Fat 6g (Saturated Fat 0.5g, Trans Fat 0g); Cholesterol 0mg; Sodium 200mg; Total Carbohydrate 11g (Dietary Fiber 2g); Protein 2g **CARBOHYDRATE CHOICES:** 1

Betty's Kitchen Tip To toast walnuts, heat oven to 350°F. Bake uncovered in ungreased shallow pan about 10 minutes, stirring occasionally, until golden brown.

Betty's Kitchen Tip If you would like to reduce the sharpness of the onion flavor, rinse the red onion under cold water and drain.

You can use a vegetable peeler to shave the asparagus and Parmesan cheese easily.

Shaved Asparagus Salad

PREP TIME: 30 Minutes / **START TO FINISH:** 30 Minutes / *6 servings*

CARB CHOICES
1/2

¼ cup fresh lemon juice

1 tablespoon Dijon mustard

2 teaspoons olive oil

½ teaspoon pepper

¼ teaspoon salt

2 cloves garlic, finely chopped

1 lb thick-stemmed fresh asparagus spears, bottom 2 inches removed, shaved into thin strips (4 cups)

1 small leek, white part only, cut into 2 (2-inch) lengths, then cut into very thin matchstick pieces

3 slices gluten-free prosciutto (from 3-oz package), cut into very thin strips

1 oz Parmesan cheese, shaved into thin strips

1 In large bowl, beat lemon juice, mustard, oil, pepper, salt and garlic with whisk.

2 Add asparagus and leek; toss to coat. Divide mixture among 6 serving plates; top with the prosciutto and cheese strips.

1 SERVING Calories 80; Total Fat 3.5g (Saturated Fat 1g, Trans Fat 0g); Cholesterol 5mg; Sodium 310mg; Total Carbohydrate 7g (Dietary Fiber 2g); Protein 5g **CARBOHYDRATE CHOICES:** ½

Betty's Kitchen Tip Choosing thicker asparagus stalks for this recipe makes them easier to shave, and will give you prettier strips.

Betty's Kitchen Tip Leeks can store a lot of sand within the layers, making them difficult to clean before cutting. Instead, cut them as called for in your recipe, then give them a bath in a bowl of cold water. Agitate them a couple of times, then lift them out, leaving the sand behind.

This beautiful riff on traditional French-style potato salad lets the tricolor potatoes shine, with loads of herbs and olive oil instead of heavy mayo.

CARB CHOICES

1½

Tricolor Potato Salad

PREP TIME: 30 Minutes / **START TO FINISH:** 40 Minutes / *12 servings*

POTATOES

- 3 lb small potato medley (white, red and purple)
- 8 cups water

DRESSING

- ½ cup extra-virgin olive oil
- ¼ cup red wine vinegar
- 1 tablespoon vegan Dijon mustard
- 1¼ teaspoons salt
- ½ teaspoon pepper
- 6 cloves garlic, finely chopped
- 10 green onions, thinly sliced (about ⅔ cup)
- ½ cup chopped fresh Italian (flat-leaf) parsley
- 1 tablespoon chopped fresh thyme leaves
- 4 cups lightly packed baby arugula

1 In 5-quart Dutch oven, place potatoes and water. Cover; heat to boiling. Reduce heat to medium-low. Simmer covered 9 to 11 minutes or until potatoes are tender when pierced with a fork. Drain potatoes; cool about 10 minutes or until cool enough to handle.

2 Meanwhile, in large bowl, beat oil, vinegar, mustard, salt, pepper and garlic with whisk until mixed. Stir in onions, parsley and thyme.

3 Cut potatoes in quarters and add to dressing in bowl; toss to coat. Spread arugula on large platter. Spoon potato mixture over arugula. Serve warm.

1 SERVING Calories 180; Total Fat 9g (Saturated Fat 1.5g, Trans Fat 0g); Cholesterol 0mg; Sodium 300mg; Total Carbohydrate 21g (Dietary Fiber 2g); Protein 3g **CARBOHYDRATE CHOICES:** 1½

Betty's Kitchen Tip Small tricolor potatoes usually come in 1½-lb bags. Want more purple? Look for similar size baby purple potatoes in bags at gourmet grocers.

Betty's Kitchen Tip Be gentle when you cut the potatoes to avoid mashing them.

Veggies sing when they are roasted, as the caramelization brings out their flavor with an added dimension.

Colorful Roasted Vegetables

PREP TIME: 15 Minutes / **START TO FINISH:** 40 Minutes / *10 servings*

- 2 tablespoons olive or canola oil
- ½ teaspoon salt
- ⅛ teaspoon pepper
- 1 clove garlic, finely chopped
- 1 cup ready-to-eat baby-cut carrots
- 6 small red potatoes, cut into quarters

- 2 small onions, cut into ½-inch wedges
- 1 small red bell pepper, seeded, cut into 1-inch pieces
- 1 medium zucchini, cut in half lengthwise, then cut crosswise into 1-inch pieces
- 1 cup grape or cherry tomatoes

1 Heat oven to 450°F. Line 15×10×1-inch pan with cooking parchment paper. In small bowl, stir oil, salt, pepper and garlic until well mixed. On pan, place carrots, potatoes, onions, bell pepper and zucchini. Drizzle with oil mixture; toss until well coated. Spread vegetables in pan in single layer.

2 Roast uncovered 20 minutes, stirring once. Stir in tomatoes. Roast about 5 minutes longer or until vegetables are tender and starting to brown.

1 SERVING Calories 130; Total Fat 3g (Saturated Fat 0g, Trans Fat 0g); Cholesterol 0mg; Sodium 140mg; Total Carbohydrate 22g (Dietary Fiber 3g); Protein 3g **CARBOHYDRATE CHOICES:** 1½

Betty's Kitchen Tip Using prepackaged baby carrots allows them to roast evenly, since they are all about the same size. If you prefer to use whole carrots, cut them into uniform pieces.

Using high, dry heat, roasting concentrates flavors and brings out the natural sweetness in vegetables.

CARB CHOICES 1

Sheet Pan–Roasted Summer Vegetables

PREP TIME: 25 Minutes / **START TO FINISH:** 55 Minutes / *8 servings*

- 2 medium zucchini, cut in half lengthwise, then cut crosswise into 1-inch pieces (about 3 cups)
- 2 medium yellow summer squash, cut in half lengthwise, then cut crosswise into 1-inch pieces (3½ cups)
- 1 medium red bell pepper, seeded, cut into 1-inch pieces (1½ cups)
- 1 medium red onion, cut into 1-inch wedges (2 cups)
- 1 cup cherry tomatoes, cut in half
- 4 tablespoons olive oil
- ¾ teaspoon salt
- ½ teaspoon pepper
- 3 cloves garlic, finely chopped
- ⅔ cup plain vegan panko crispy bread crumbs
- 2 teaspoons lemon zest
- ¼ cup chopped fresh basil leaves

1 Heat oven to 450°F. Spray 18×13-inch half-sheet pan with cooking spray.

2 On sheet pan, combine zucchini, summer squash, bell pepper, onion and tomatoes. Drizzle with 2 tablespoons of the oil, ½ teaspoon of the salt and the pepper; toss until vegetables are coated.

3 Roast uncovered 25 to 30 minutes, stirring after 15 minutes, or until vegetables are tender and just starting to brown.

4 Meanwhile, in 8-inch skillet, heat 1 tablespoon of the oil over medium heat. Add garlic; cook and stir 1 minute or until fragrant. Remove garlic to small bowl. Add remaining 1 tablespoon oil to skillet; heat over medium heat. Add bread crumbs; stir to coat. Cook and stir 2 to 3 minutes or until lightly browned. Spoon into bowl with garlic; stir in lemon zest and remaining ¼ teaspoon salt. Sprinkle bread crumb mixture and basil over roasted vegetables before serving.

1 SERVING Calories 140; Total Fat 7g (Saturated Fat 1g, Trans Fat 0g); Cholesterol 0mg; Sodium 320mg; Total Carbohydrate 15g (Dietary Fiber 2g); Protein 3g **CARBOHYDRATE CHOICES: 1**

Betty's Kitchen Tip Chopped basil tends to turn dark over time, so it's best to chop the basil just before serving.

Who wouldn't want to eat more veggies when they look and taste this delicious? Developed to be a board, this recipe shows off the fun shapes and colors of the roasted vegetables.

CARB CHOICES

1

Roasted Vegetables with Smoky Sour Cream and Chive Dip

PREP TIME: 35 Minutes / **START TO FINISH:** 1 Hour / *6 servings* (¾ *cup vegetables and about 2 tablespoons dip each*)

ROASTED VEGETABLES

- 1 broccoli crown (about 1.3 lb)
- 1 large sweet potato, peeled, cut in half lengthwise, then crosswise into ½-inch pieces (2 cups)
- 1 bunch radishes, trimmed, cut in half (1 cup)
- 2 orange or yellow bell peppers, cut into ½-inch rings
- 1 package (8 oz) fresh whole mushrooms
- 1 tablespoon chopped fresh rosemary leaves
- 1 teaspoon lemon zest
- ¼ teaspoon salt
- ¼ teaspoon crushed red pepper flakes

SMOKY SOUR CREAM AND CHIVE DIP

- ⅔ cup vegan light sour cream alternative
- ¼ cup chopped fresh chives or finely chopped green onion (4 medium)
- ½ teaspoon smoked paprika
- ⅛ teaspoon salt
  Additional chopped chives, if desired

1 Move oven racks to upper and lower thirds of oven. Heat oven to 425°F. Spray two 15×10×2-inch pans with cooking spray.

2 Trim ½ inch off broccoli stems; peel stems, if desired. Cut stems with florets into ½-inch-wide stalks. Divide vegetables between pans, being careful to keep each type of vegetable together on pan. Spray with cooking spray. In small bowl, stir together rosemary, lemon zest, salt and red pepper flakes. Sprinkle evenly over vegetables.

3 Roast 20 to 25 minutes or until vegetables are crisp and beginning to brown, turning vegetables and rotating pans between racks after about 10 minutes.

4 Meanwhile, in small bowl, stir together all dip ingredients, except additional chives. Sprinkle with additional chives.

5 Arrange vegetables on board or large platter, scraping any seasoning or juice left on pan over vegetables. Serve with dip.

1 SERVING Calories 100; Total Fat 3.5g (Saturated Fat 2g, Trans Fat 0g); Cholesterol 10mg; Sodium 210mg; Total Carbohydrate 14g (Dietary Fiber 3g); Protein 3g **CARBOHYDRATE CHOICES:** 1

Pair leftover veggies with a little sliced cooked chicken breast for a tasty Asian-inspired salad lunch.

Stir-Fry Vegetables with Spicy Sesame Sauce

PREP TIME: 15 Minutes / **START TO FINISH:** 15 Minutes / *4 servings*

- 1 cup fresh snow pea pods, strings removed
- 1 cup thinly sliced red bell pepper (1 medium)
- 1 medium yellow onion, sliced (1 cup)
- ½ cup coarsely shredded carrot (about 1 medium)
- ½ cup shredded red cabbage
- 1 tablespoon gluten-free soy sauce
- ½ teaspoon Asian chili garlic sauce or harissa
- ½ teaspoon toasted sesame oil
- 1 teaspoon toasted sesame seed

1 In 8-inch square (2-quart) microwavable baking dish, mix snow pea pods, bell pepper, onion, carrot and cabbage. Cover with plastic wrap, folding back one corner ¼ inch to vent steam. Microwave on High 5 to 6 minutes or until vegetables are crisp-tender.

2 Meanwhile, in small bowl, mix soy sauce, chili garlic sauce and sesame oil.

3 Carefully remove plastic wrap. Drizzle soy mixture over vegetables; toss to coat. Top with sesame seed.

1 SERVING Calories 50; Total Fat 1.5g (Saturated Fat 0g, Trans Fat 0g); Cholesterol 0mg; Sodium 250mg; Total Carbohydrate 8g (Dietary Fiber 2g); Protein 2g **CARBOHYDRATE CHOICES:** ½

Betty's Kitchen Tip Save yourself some time in the kitchen by using preshredded carrot and cabbage.

Betty's Kitchen Tip Either chile garlic sauce or harissa will add some spice and heat to these veggies. Harissa comes in both mild and spicy varieties—feel free to choose the level of heat you want. Look for them in the international ingredients aisle of your grocery store.

A perfect partner for grilled or broiled chicken, pork chops or burgers, any leftovers from this savory combination could be the star of your salad bowl lunch the next day.

Roasted Asparagus with Mushrooms and Walnuts

PREP TIME: 15 Minutes / **START TO FINISH:** 30 Minutes / *4 servings*

1 lb fresh asparagus

2 cups sliced fresh mushrooms (from 8-oz package)

¼ cup thinly sliced red onion

3 tablespoons chopped walnuts

1 tablespoon chopped fresh rosemary leaves

½ teaspoon garlic-pepper blend

1 tablespoon olive oil

1 Heat oven to 425°F. Wash asparagus. Break off tough ends where stalks snap easily; discard ends.

2 On 15×10×1-inch pan, arrange asparagus, mushrooms and onion. Sprinkle with walnuts, rosemary and garlic-pepper blend; drizzle with olive oil.

3 Roast uncovered 14 to 16 minutes or until asparagus is crisp-tender. Serve warm or at room temperature.

1 SERVING Calories 100; Total Fat 7g (Saturated Fat 1g, Trans Fat 0g); Cholesterol 0mg; Sodium 55mg; Total Carbohydrate 5g (Dietary Fiber 2g); Protein 3g **CARBOHYDRATE CHOICES:** ½

This spinach has so much flavor from coconut milk and garlic, you won't even miss the dairy you'd find in traditional creamed spinach. Don't skip the lemon squeeze at the end—it brightens everything up and makes this dish irresistible.

CARB CHOICES

1/2

Creamy Garlic Spinach

PREP TIME: 25 Minutes / **START TO FINISH:** 25 Minutes / *8 servings (½ cup each)*

- 2 tablespoons virgin coconut oil
- 1 medium onion, chopped (1 cup)
- 1 small red bell pepper, chopped (¾ cup)
- 4 cloves garlic, finely chopped
- ¾ teaspoon salt
- ½ teaspoon crushed red pepper flakes
- 4 packages (5 oz each) baby spinach leaves
- ½ cup unsweetened coconut milk (from 13.66-oz can; not cream of coconut)
- Lemon wedges

1 In a 4-quart saucepan, heat coconut oil over medium heat. Cook onion and bell pepper in oil 6 to 7 minutes, stirring frequently, or until tender. Add garlic, salt and red pepper flakes; cook and stir 1 minute.

2 Gradually add spinach. Cook, stirring, just until spinach is wilted. Stir in coconut milk; cook just until heated. Serve with lemon wedges.

1 SERVING Calories 100; Total Fat 7g (Saturated Fat 6g, Trans Fat 0g); Cholesterol 0mg; Sodium 280mg; Total Carbohydrate 7g (Dietary Fiber 2g); Protein 2g **CARBOHYDRATE CHOICES:** ½

Betty's Kitchen Tip Canned coconut milk can sometimes separate in storage, leaving a thick layer of rich coconut milk on top and a watery liquid on the bottom. The easiest way to recombine them is to pour the coconut milk into a large measuring cup or medium bowl and beat with a whisk until mixed. Pour any unused coconut milk in a covered refrigerator- or freezer-safe storage container; refrigerate or freeze. Use refrigerated coconut milk within 1 week or frozen coconut milk within 1 month (thaw in refrigerator before using). Whisk coconut milk until well blended before you use it.

Betty's Kitchen Tip Coconut oil comes in two varieties: virgin and refined. Virgin coconut oil is made using a cold-press process, and retains more coconut flavor. Refined oil is more processed and is essentially free of odor or flavor.

Those who like their collards meltingly tender should let the greens stew together with the ham bone and other ingredients for 6 hours, while those who prefer a more toothsome texture can stop cooking after 4 hours.

CARB CHOICES

$1/2$

Collard Greens with Ham

PREP TIME: 30 Minutes / **START TO FINISH:** 4 Hours 30 Minutes / *8 servings (¾ cup each)*

- 2 **tablespoons canola oil**
- 1 **cooked ham bone (1 to 2 lb) with the meat still attached after carving**
- 2 **cups thinly sliced onion (1 large)**
- ½ **teaspoon crushed red pepper flakes**
- 5 **cloves garlic, chopped**

- 1 **tablespoon packed brown sugar**
- 2 **cups gluten-free chicken broth (for homemade broth, see page 12)**
- 1½ **lb collard greens, ribs removed, cut in 1-inch-wide strips (about 3 bunches)**
- 1 **teaspoon apple cider vinegar**

1 Spray 6-quart slow cooker with cooking spray. In 12-inch skillet, heat 1 tablespoon of the oil over medium heat until hot. Cook ham bone in oil 4 to 6 minutes, turning several times, or until browned on all sides. Transfer to slow cooker.

2 Add remaining tablespoon of vegetable oil to same skillet. Add onion and red pepper flakes; cook over medium heat 2 to 4 minutes, stirring frequently, or until onion begins to brown. Add garlic and brown sugar; cook 1 minute. Stir in broth; heat just to simmering. Stir in greens a few handfuls at a time until wilted slightly.

3 Pour mixture around ham bone in slow cooker. Cover; cook on Low heat setting 4 to 6 hours or until collards reach desired tenderness. Remove bone. Remove meat from bone, chop and stir into greens. Stir in vinegar.

1 SERVING Calories 150; Total Fat 7g (Saturated Fat 1.5g, Trans Fat 0g); Cholesterol 25mg; Sodium 220mg; Total Carbohydrate 10g (Dietary Fiber 4g); Protein 11g **CARBOHYDRATE CHOICES:** ½

Betty's Kitchen Tip Collards are a loose-leaf variety of cabbage with flavor that's a cross between cabbage and kale. To prepare collards, wash them well. Remove thick ribs from center by holding each leaf with one hand and stripping away rib with other hand. Then layer several leaves in a stack, roll up lengthwise and cut into 1-inch-wide slices.

Betty's Kitchen Tip If you've ever wondered what to do with the bone from your holiday ham, this is the perfect use. If you're not planning to make collards right away, store the ham bone in a resealable freezer plastic bag up to 3 months. Thaw in refrigerator the night before using.

Crumb-Topped Greens

Choose whatever greens you like, what you have on hand or what's on sale! This recipe cooks them just until they are tender, with a few flavorful seasonings to make them shine. Try the microwave version when it's too hot to cook.

CARB CHOICES

$1/2$

Garlicky Greens

PREP TIME: 15 Minutes / **START TO FINISH:** 25 Minutes / *6 servings ($1/2$ cup each)*

1 pound kale leaves, or beet or collard greens

1 tablespoon olive oil

4 cloves garlic, chopped

4 green onions, thinly sliced ($1/4$ cup)

$1/4$ cup water

$1/4$ to $1/2$ teaspoon crushed red pepper flakes

2 teaspoons fresh lemon juice

$1/2$ teaspoon salt

1 SERVING Calories 70; Total Fat 3g (Saturated Fat 0g, Trans Fat 0g); Cholesterol 0mg; Sodium 230mg; Total Carbohydrate 8g (Dietary Fiber 3g); Protein 3g **CARBOHYDRATE CHOICES:** $1/2$

1 SERVING (CRUMB-TOPPED GREENS) Calories 100; Total Fat 6g (Saturated Fat 1.5g, Trans Fat 0g); Cholesterol 5mg; Sodium 300mg; Total Carbohydrate 9g (Dietary Fiber 3g); Protein 3g **CARBOHYDRATE CHOICES:** $1/2$

1 Prep the kale, removing root ends and imperfect leaves. Wash several times in water, lifting out each time; drain, leaving water on the leaves. Remove and discard kale or collard ribs and tough beet stems. Coarsely chop leaves.

2 In 12-inch nonstick skillet, heat oil over medium heat. Add garlic and onions and cook about 1 minute. Add greens, water and red pepper flakes; toss to coat greens. Cover; cook over low heat: kale 4 to 6 minutes or beet or collard greens 8 to 10 minutes, or until tender, stirring once.

3 Add lemon juice and salt; toss lightly to mix.

Crumb-Topped Greens In small skillet, melt 1 tablespoon butter over medium heat. Stir in $1/3$ cup dry bread crumbs. Cook and stir until golden brown. Remove from heat; let cool while preparing greens. Serve crumbs over cooked greens.

To Steam In saucepan or deep skillet, place steamer basket in $1/2$ inch of water (water should not touch bottom of basket.) Place greens in basket. Cover; heat to boiling; reduce heat to low. Steam 5 to 8 minutes or until tender.

To Microwave Place greens in 2-quart microwavable bowl or baking dish with 2 tablespoons water. Cover with plastic wrap. Microwave on High until tender: beet greens, chicory or escarole 8 to 10 minutes; collards, kale, mustard, spinach, Swiss chard or turnip greens 4 to 6 minutes.

Roasting enhances carrots' natural sweetness, and a bit of balsamic vinegar brings the right amount of zippy tartness to this easy, attractive dish.

CARB CHOICES

1

Honey-Balsamic Roasted Carrots

PREP TIME: 15 Minutes / **START TO FINISH:** 45 Minutes / *8 servings*

2 tablespoons butter, melted

2 tablespoons balsamic vinegar

2 tablespoons honey

½ teaspoon salt

¼ teaspoon pepper

1 bag (2 lb) fresh carrots, peeled, quartered lengthwise

2 tablespoons chopped fresh Italian (flat-leaf) parsley

1 Heat oven to 400°F. Spray 18×13-inch half-sheet pan with cooking spray.

2 In small bowl, mix butter, 1 tablespoon of the vinegar, the honey, salt and pepper until blended. Place carrots on pan. Top with butter mixture; toss to coat. Spread carrots in single layer.

3 Roast uncovered 15 minutes; stir. Roast 13 to 18 minutes longer or until carrots are tender and browned. Drizzle with remaining 1 tablespoon vinegar. Stir carrots in pan; immediately remove carrots from pan. Top with parsley.

1 SERVING Calories 90; Total Fat 3g (Saturated Fat 2g, Trans Fat 0g); Cholesterol 10mg; Sodium 240mg; Total Carbohydrate 15g (Dietary Fiber 3g); Protein 1g **CARBOHYDRATE CHOICES:** 1

Betty's Kitchen Tip If your carrots are very thin, cut them in half lengthwise instead of quarters.

Roasted carrots are sprinkled with cumin and topped with a hint of orange zest for an unexpectedly delicious burst of flavor.

CARB CHOICES

1

Cumin-Citrus Roasted Carrots

PREP TIME: 10 Minutes / **START TO FINISH:** 40 Minutes / *6 servings*

1 bag (2 lb) fresh carrots, peeled, cut diagonally into 2-inch pieces

2 tablespoons olive oil

1 teaspoon ground cumin

½ teaspoon salt

¼ teaspoon pepper

1 tablespoon chopped fresh chives

1 teaspoon orange zest

1 Heat oven to 400°F. Spray 15×10×1-inch pan with cooking spray.

2 In large bowl, stir carrots, olive oil, cumin, salt and pepper until well coated. Spread in pan in single layer.

3 Roast 25 to 30 minutes, stirring halfway through, or until tender and browned. Toss carrots with chives and orange zest before serving.

1 SERVING Calories 100; Total Fat 5g (Saturated Fat 0.5g, Trans Fat 0g); Cholesterol 0mg; Sodium 290mg; Total Carbohydrate 13g (Dietary Fiber 4g); Protein 1g **CARBOHYDRATE CHOICES:** 1

Betty's Kitchen Tip Carrot pieces should be of equal size and width for even roasting. If some carrots are wider than average, cut them in half lengthwise before cutting into pieces.

Betty's Kitchen Tip Use multicolored carrots for a beautiful twist on this recipe.

Don't skip crisping the sage—it really takes this dish to the next level. You can leave the sage leaves whole or crumble if you like, so the rich, buttery herbal flavor is in every bite.

CARB CHOICES

1

Creamy Butternut Squash

PREP TIME: 15 Minutes / **START TO FINISH:** 1 Hour 25 Minutes / *8 servings (about ½ cup each)*

- 1 (3- to 4-lb) butternut squash, quartered, seeded
- 1 tablespoon butter
- 5 medium fresh sage leaves
- 1 clove garlic, finely chopped
- 1 teaspoon fresh thyme leaves
- ¼ teaspoon salt
- ⅛ teaspoon crushed red pepper flakes
- 2 oz cream cheese, cubed and softened (from 8-oz package)
- ¼ cup shredded Parmesan cheese (1 oz)

1 SERVING Calories 110; Total Fat 5g (Saturated Fat 3g, Trans Fat 0g); Cholesterol 15mg; Sodium 150mg; Total Carbohydrate 14g (Dietary Fiber 4g); Protein 3g **CARBOHYDRATE CHOICES:** 1

Betty's Kitchen Tip Roasted butternut squash is so tender it virtually purees itself as it's scooped from its skin. But if you prefer a super-smooth, velvety texture, make the extra effort to puree the mixture in a blender or food processor.

1 Heat oven to 425°F. Spray 13×9-inch baking dish with cooking spray. Place squash cut side down in dish.

2 Roast uncovered 55 to 60 minutes or until squash is tender. Let stand 10 minutes. Using spoon, scoop flesh from squash into heatproof medium bowl. Discard skin.

3 In 4-quart saucepan, melt butter over medium heat. Add sage; cook 2 to 3 minutes or until crisp. Using slotted spoon, transfer to paper towel–lined plate.

4 Add garlic, thyme, salt and pepper flakes to same saucepan; cook over medium heat 30 seconds. Stir in squash, breaking up with spoon; cook 2 to 3 minutes, stirring occasionally, or until squash is hot. Remove from heat. Add cream cheese and Parmesan cheese; stir until cheeses are melted. Spoon into 1-quart heatproof serving dish; top with sage.

Multi Cooker Directions In 6-quart multi cooker insert, place 1 cup water. Place rack in insert. Place squash on top of rack. Secure lid; set pressure valve to SEALING. Select MANUAL; cook on high pressure 16 minutes. Select CANCEL. Set pressure valve to VENTING to quick-release pressure. Place squash on cutting board. Remove rack, and drain off cooking liquid. When cool enough to handle, using spoon, scrape squash flesh from skin. Set aside. Select SAUTE; adjust to normal. Melt butter in insert. Add sage; cook 1 to 2 minutes or until crisp. Using slotted spoon, transfer to paper towel–lined plate. Add garlic, thyme, salt and pepper flakes; cook 30 seconds. Stir in squash; cook 1 to 2 minutes, breaking up with rubber spatula, until smooth. Select CANCEL. Add cream cheese and Parmesan cheese; stir until cheeses are melted. Top with sage.

Starting with a bag of riced cauliflower makes this one-dish fried "rice" easy to prepare and a terrific way to get more veggies into your day.

CARB CHOICES
1

Cauliflower Fried "Rice"

PREP TIME: 30 Minutes / **START TO FINISH:** 30 Minutes / *4 servings (1 cup each)*

1 tablespoon olive oil

1 small onion, chopped (½ cup)

1 clove garlic, finely chopped

1 bag (12 oz) frozen riced cauliflower

1 cup frozen peas and carrots (from 10-oz bag)

½ cup diced red bell pepper

2 tablespoons gluten-free reduced-sodium soy sauce

1 tablespoon gluten-free hoisin sauce

2 eggs, beaten

2 tablespoons sliced green onions (2 medium)

1 In 12-inch skillet, heat oil over medium-high heat. Add onion and garlic. Cook 1 to 3 minutes, stirring occasionally, or until onion begins to brown. Reduce heat to medium; stir in cauliflower, peas and carrots and bell pepper. Cover; cook 9 to 12 minutes, stirring occasionally, or until vegetables are crisp-tender.

2 Meanwhile, in small bowl, mix soy sauce and hoisin sauce; set aside.

3 Stir eggs into mixture in skillet; cook 1 to 2 minutes or until eggs are cooked. Remove from heat; stir in sauce. Top with green onions.

1 SERVING Calories 140; Total Fat 7g (Saturated Fat 1.5g, Trans Fat 0g); Cholesterol 95mg; Sodium 420mg; Total Carbohydrate 12g (Dietary Fiber 4g); Protein 7g **CARBOHYDRATE CHOICES:** 1

Betty's Kitchen Tip Hoisin is a Chinese condiment frequently used in stir-fries and other dishes to add a rich, complex depth of flavor with its ingredient blend, including five-spice powder and star anise. Look for it near the other Asian ingredients in your grocery store.

Spiralizers are a great way to turn veggies into "noodles." Some stores carry spiralized veggies in the refrigerated section of the produce department. To make your own, straight, even vegetables work the best. If you don't have a spiralizer, use a vegetable peeler: Pull the peeler down the sides of the squash to make long strips. When you reach the seedy core, rotate the squash and repeat. The baking time may be less.

CARB CHOICES

0

Spiral Summer Squash

PREP TIME: 10 Minutes / **START TO FINISH:** 20 Minutes / *4 servings*

1 (6-inch-long) zucchini
1 (6-inch-long) yellow summer squash

2 teaspoons olive oil
¼ teaspoon salt
Pepper, if desired

1 Heat oven to 400°F. Line 15×10×1-inch pan with foil.

2 Cut off ends of both squash. Cut squash with spiralizer according to manufacturer's directions. Place in pan. Drizzle with oil; sprinkle with salt. Toss to coat; spread squash in single layer.

3 Bake 8 to 10 minutes or just until tender. Sprinkle with pepper.

1 SERVING Calories 40; Total Fat 2.5g (Saturated Fat 0g, Trans Fat 0g); Cholesterol 0mg; Sodium 150mg; Total Carbohydrate 3g (Dietary Fiber 1g); Protein 1g **CARBOHYDRATE CHOICES:** 0

Satisfying
Dinners

For extra flavor, consider drizzling slices of pizza with an additional tablespoon of salsa, or sprinkling them with red pepper flakes, for very little "cost," nutritionally speaking.

CARB CHOICES
2½

Chicken Taco Pizza

PREP TIME: 45 Minutes / **START TO FINISH:** 1 Hour 35 Minutes / *8 servings (2 slices each)*

PIZZA CRUST

- 2½ to 3 cups whole wheat flour
- 1 tablespoon sugar
- 1 teaspoon salt
- 1 package regular active or fast-acting dry yeast (2¼ teaspoons)
- 1 cup very warm water (120°F to 130°F)
- 3 tablespoons olive oil or canola oil
- 2 teaspoons cornmeal

PIZZA TOPPINGS

- 1 cup reduced-sodium refried beans
- 1 cup Salsa (page 41)
- 2 cups chopped cooked chicken (for homemade chicken, see page 12)
- 1½ cups shredded cheddar cheese (6 oz)
- 4 cups shredded lettuce (½ medium head)
- 1 small tomato, chopped
- 1 avocado, pitted, peeled and sliced

1 In large bowl, mix 1 cup of the flour, the sugar, salt and yeast. Add water and oil. Beat with electric mixer on medium speed 3 minutes, scraping bowl frequently. Stir the remaining flour, ½ cup at a time, just until dough is soft and leaves side of bowl. Place dough on lightly floured surface; knead about 5 minutes or until dough is smooth and springy.

2 Cover loosely with plastic wrap and let rest 30 minutes.

3 **For Thin Crusts:** Heat oven to 425°F. Grease cookie sheet or pizza pan with oil and sprinkle with cornmeal. Divide dough in half. Pat each half of dough into 12-inch circle on cookie sheet. Bake 7 to 8 minutes or until crust just begins to brown.

For Thick Crusts: Grease two 8-inch square or 9-inch round baking pans with oil. Sprinkle with cornmeal. Divide dough in half. Pat each half into bottom of pan using floured fingers. Cover loosely with plastic wrap; let rise in warm place 30 to 45 minutes or until almost doubled in size. Move oven rack to lowest position. Heat oven to 375°F. Bake 20 to 22 minutes or until crust begins to brown.

4 Spoon refried beans evenly over crusts. Spoon salsa, chicken and cheese evenly over beans. Bake thin-crust pizzas 8 to 10 minutes; bake thick-crust pizzas 18 to 20 minutes; both until cheese is melted. Top with lettuce, tomato and avocado. Cut into wedges to serve.

1 SERVING Calories 410; Total Fat 19g (Saturated Fat 6g, Trans Fat 0g); Cholesterol 50mg; Sodium 550mg; Total Carbohydrate 38g (Dietary Fiber 7g); Protein 22g **CARBOHYDRATE CHOICES:** 2½

Make Ahead **To refrigerate:** After Step 2, place dough in greased bowl; cover tightly with plastic wrap. Refrigerate up to 4 days. Continue as directed in Step 3. **To freeze:** After Step 2, shape into 2 balls. Wrap each ball tightly in plastic wrap. Freeze up to 2 months. To use, thaw in refrigerator 4 to 6 hours. Continue as directed in Step 3.

In India or Pakistan, *korma* traditionally refers to a dish made with mutton, lamb or chicken, onions and possibly other vegetables in a sauce with yogurt, curry and other spices. This is a super-easy version for a weeknight dinner.

Quick Skillet Chicken Korma

PREP TIME: 20 Minutes / **START TO FINISH:** 20 Minutes / *4 servings (about ½ cup each)*

- 1 tablespoon canola oil
- 1 lb boneless skinless chicken breasts, cut into ¾-inch cubes
- 1 small onion, chopped (½ cup)
- 1 teaspoon garam masala
- ½ teaspoon curry powder
- ½ teaspoon salt
- ⅛ to ¼ teaspoon ground red pepper (cayenne)
- ½ cup water
- ⅔ cup plain low-fat yogurt
- 2 cups hot cooked basmati or regular long-grain white rice
- 2 tablespoons chopped fresh cilantro

1 SERVING Calories 290; Total Fat 8g (Saturated Fat 2g, Trans Fat 0g); Cholesterol 75mg; Sodium 690mg; Total Carbohydrate 26g (Dietary Fiber 1g); Protein 29g **CARBOHYDRATE CHOICES:** 2

Betty's Kitchen Tip Boneless skinless chicken thighs work just as well as breasts in this recipe.

Betty's Kitchen Tip Garam masala is an Indian spice blend that usually consists of cumin, coriander, cinnamon, cloves, cardamom, peppercorns, bay leaves and sometimes other spices.

1 Spray 12-inch skillet with cooking spray. Add oil to skillet; heat over medium-high heat until hot. Add chicken; cook 2 to 3 minutes without stirring or until chicken releases easily from skillet. Stir in onion, garam masala, curry powder, salt and red pepper. Cook 3 minutes, stirring frequently.

2 Stir in water; heat to simmering over high heat. Reduce heat; cook 4 to 5 minutes longer or until chicken is no longer pink in center and sauce is reduced by half. Remove from heat; let stand 1 minute. Stir in yogurt. Serve over rice; top with cilantro.

This tender chicken in a luscious sauce might look like it came from a nice restaurant, but it's a dish you can cook up in your own kitchen without a lot of fuss or time.

Lemon-Dijon Chicken Skillet

PREP TIME: 25 Minutes / **START TO FINISH:** 45 Minutes / *6 servings (1 thigh and ¼ cup sauce each)*

3 teaspoons Dijon mustard

1 teaspoon finely chopped fresh rosemary plus 2 sprigs rosemary

2 teaspoons fresh lemon juice

4 cloves garlic, finely chopped

6 bone-in chicken thighs (about 1½ lb total)

¼ teaspoon salt

1 tablespoon canola oil

½ cup finely chopped onion (1 small)

½ cup dry white wine (such as sauvignon blanc)

1½ cups reduced-sodium chicken broth (for homemade broth, see page 12)

1 tablespoon butter

1 tablespoon all-purpose flour

1 tablespoon chopped Italian (flat-leaf) parsley

1 In small bowl, mix 2 teaspoons of the mustard, the chopped rosemary, 1 teaspoon of the lemon juice and the garlic. Rub mixture all over chicken thighs; season with salt.

2 In 12-inch nonstick skillet, heat oil over medium heat. Add chicken thighs; cook 4 minutes on each side or until brown. Add onion; cook 2 to 3 minutes or until just softened. Add wine; stir to loosen browned bits from bottom of pan. Add broth and rosemary sprigs. Increase heat to medium-high and heat to boiling. Reduce heat, cover and simmer 10 to 13 minutes or until juice of chicken is clear when thickest part is cut to bone and instant-read meat thermometer reads 165°F. Remove chicken to plate and keep warm.

3 Strain cooking liquid through fine-mesh strainer into small heatproof bowl; discard solids. Heat butter in same skillet over medium heat. Stir in flour until smooth; cook 1 minute, stirring constantly, or until mixture is lightly browned and bubbling. Slowly add cooking liquid; beat with whisk to combine. Add remaining 1 teaspoon mustard and remaining 1 teaspoon lemon juice; cook 1 to 2 minutes or until slightly thickened. Spoon some of sauce over chicken; top with parsley. Serve remaining sauce on the side.

1 SERVING Calories 160; Total Fat 9g (Saturated Fat 2.5g, Trans Fat 0g); Cholesterol 80mg; Sodium 300mg; Total Carbohydrate 3g (Dietary Fiber 0g); Protein 16g **CARBOHYDRATE CHOICES:** 0

Betty's Kitchen Tip If you prefer not to cook with wine, an extra ½ cup chicken broth makes the perfect substitute.

Betty's Kitchen Tip Garnish with lemon slices if desired.

Use the remaining salsa to make a great green gazpacho lunch soup or snack. Or create a Mexican-inspired bowl with cooked chicken, brown rice, black beans, chopped tomatoes and some of the salsa. Cover and store the remaining salsa in the refrigerator to use within 3 days.

CARB CHOICES 2

Fiesta Lime Chicken Tacos

PREP TIME: 1 Hour / **START TO FINISH:** 2 Hours 10 Minutes / *5 servings (2 tacos each)*

CHICKEN
- 2 teaspoons lime zest
- 2 tablespoons fresh lime juice
- 1 tablespoon water
- 1 tablespoon canola oil
- 1 tablespoon honey
- 1 package (0.85 oz) chicken taco seasoning mix
- 1 package (20 oz) boneless skinless chicken breasts
- Grilling spray

SALSA VERDE
- 1½ lb tomatillos, husks removed, cored, cut in quarters (4½ cups)
- 1 small onion, chopped (½ cup)
- ¼ cup chopped fresh cilantro
- 2 cloves garlic, chopped
- 1 tablespoon chopped seeded jalapeño chile
- 1 tablespoon fresh lime juice
- ½ teaspoon salt

TACOS
- 1 package (4.7 oz) taco shells that stand on their own
- ¾ cup shredded lettuce
- ¾ cup chopped tomatoes

1 In 1-gallon resealable food-storage plastic bag, mix all chicken ingredients except chicken and grilling spray. Add chicken; seal bag. Shake until chicken is evenly coated. Refrigerate at least 1 hour but no longer than 2 hours.

2 Meanwhile, in food processor, place all salsa ingredients. Cover; process about 1 minute, using quick on-and-off pulses, or until blended. In 10-inch nonstick skillet, heat tomatillo mixture over medium-high heat 6 to 8 minutes, stirring occasionally, or until mixture boils and thickens. Pour into small heatproof bowl; refrigerate at least 1 hour or until cool.

3 Spray gas or charcoal grill with grilling spray. Heat grill to medium.

4 Drain chicken and discard any remaining marinade. Place chicken on grill over medium heat. Cover grill; cook 12 to 15 minutes, turning once, or until juice of chicken is clear when center of thickest part is cut and instant-read meat thermometer reads 165°F. Let stand 5 minutes before cutting into slices.

5 Heat taco shells as directed on package. Divide chicken pieces evenly among shells. Top each taco with 2 tablespoons salsa verde and generous 1 tablespoon each lettuce and tomato.

1 SERVING Calories 380; Total Fat 14g (Saturated Fat 4g, Trans Fat 0g); Cholesterol 70mg; Sodium 750mg; Total Carbohydrate 35g (Dietary Fiber 6g); Protein 29g **CARBOHYDRATE CHOICES:** 2

Betty's Kitchen Tip Tomatillos are in the same family as tomatoes but are very different. They are green when ripe, with a flavor that hints of lemon and apples. Tomatillos have a thick skin with a papery covering, and a firm texture much like an unripe, green tomato. To prepare, open the dry husks, pull up toward top of tomatillo and remove. Rinse tomatillos and rub gently to remove sticky film.

So that your chicken comes out moist and tender, in the first step cook it just until the outside is no longer pink. It will continue to cook as the rice cooks, so everything will be done at the same time.

CARB CHOICES 3

Hawaiian Chicken

PREP TIME: 20 Minutes / **START TO FINISH:** 50 Minutes / *5 servings (about 1¼ cups each)*

- 1 tablespoon canola oil
- 1 lb boneless skinless chicken breasts, cut into bite-size pieces
- 2 medium bell peppers (any color), seeded, coarsely chopped (2 cups)
- 1 medium onion, cut into wedges
- 1 can (8 oz) pineapple chunks in juice, drained, juice reserved
- 1 cup uncooked regular long-grain white rice
- 1 cup reduced-fat (lite) coconut milk (from 14-oz can; not cream of coconut)
- ⅔ cup chicken broth (from 32-oz carton)
- ¾ teaspoon salt
- 1 tablespoon chopped fresh cilantro
- ½ cup unsalted cashew halves and pieces
- 4 medium green onions, sliced (¼ cup)

1 In 12-inch skillet, heat oil over medium-high heat. Add chicken, bell peppers and onion wedges; cook 3 to 4 minutes, stirring frequently, or until chicken is no longer pink.

2 Stir in reserved pineapple juice, rice, coconut milk, chicken broth and salt. Heat to boiling; reduce heat to low. Cover; simmer 20 to 25 minutes, stirring once, or until rice is tender and liquid is absorbed.

3 Stir in pineapple chunks and cilantro; cook until thoroughly heated. Sprinkle with cashews and green onions.

1 SERVING Calories 430; Total Fat 15g (Saturated Fat 5g, Trans Fat 0g); Cholesterol 55mg; Sodium 540mg; Total Carbohydrate 47g (Dietary Fiber 3g); Protein 27g **CARBOHYDRATE CHOICES:** 3

If you have leftover gingerroot after making this recipe, steep slices in hot water for a spicy pick-me-up "tea."

CARB CHOICES 2

Grilled Sriracha Chicken with Garlic-Cilantro Rice

PREP TIME: 20 Minutes / **START TO FINISH:** 55 Minutes / *4 servings*

CHICKEN
- 8 (8-inch) bamboo skewers
- 1 tablespoon sriracha sauce
- 1 tablespoon reduced-sodium soy sauce
- 1 teaspoon grated gingerroot
- 1 teaspoon canola oil
- 1 lb boneless skinless chicken breasts, cut into 32 pieces, about 1½ inches each

Grilling spray
Lime wedges

RICE
- ¾ cup uncooked regular long-grain white rice
- 1½ cups water
- 3 cloves garlic, finely chopped
- ⅛ teaspoon salt
- ⅓ cup chopped fresh cilantro

1 Soak skewers in water 15 minutes.

2 In medium bowl, mix sriracha sauce, soy sauce, gingerroot and oil. Add chicken; toss to coat. On each skewer, thread 4 pieces of chicken. Place on plate, cover and refrigerate until you're ready to grill.

3 In 1-quart saucepan, heat rice, water, garlic and salt to boiling over high heat. Stir; reduce heat to low. Cover; cook 15 minutes. Remove from heat; let stand 5 minutes. Fluff with fork; stir in cilantro. Cover to keep warm.

4 Meanwhile, spray gas or charcoal grill with grilling spray. Heat grill to medium. Place chicken skewers on grill over medium heat. Cover grill; cook 8 to 10 minutes, turning skewers occasionally to cook on all sides, or until chicken is no longer pink in center.

5 Serve skewers over rice with lime wedges.

1 SERVING Calories 290; Total Fat 5g (Saturated Fat 1g, Trans Fat 0g); Cholesterol 70mg; Sodium 390mg; Total Carbohydrate 32g (Dietary Fiber 0g); Protein 29g **CARBOHYDRATE CHOICES:** 2

Betty's Kitchen Tip If the weather doesn't cooperate with your grilling plans, cook these skewers indoors on a grill pan. Heat the pan over medium heat. You may need to add a couple of minutes to the cook time.

The sensational flavors of Middle Eastern shawarma will soon become family favorites after you try this quick, healthful recipe.

CARB CHOICES

1½

Chicken Shawarma Meatball Pitas

PREP TIME: 40 Minutes / **START TO FINISH:** 40 Minutes / *8 servings*

MEATBALLS

- 3 tablespoons low-sodium chicken broth
- 2 tablespoons sesame tahini paste
- 1 tablespoon honey
- 1 teaspoon ground ginger
- 1 teaspoon ground allspice
- ½ teaspoon salt
- ½ teaspoon ground red pepper (cayenne)
- 1 lb ground chicken breast

YOGURT SAUCE

- 1 cup plain fat-free yogurt
- ½ cup finely chopped onion (1 small)
- ¼ teaspoon salt

PITAS

- 4 cups shredded lettuce (½ medium head)
- 4 (6-inch) whole wheat pita (pocket) breads, cut in half, toasted
- 2 tomatoes, diced
- 2 tablespoons chopped fresh cilantro

1 Heat oven to 375° F. Line 15×10×1-inch pan with foil; spray with cooking spray.

2 In large bowl, mix all meatball ingredients except chicken until blended. Add chicken and mix well. Shape into 16 (1½-inch) balls. Place on pan.

3 Bake 12 to 15 minutes or until instant-read meat thermometer inserted in center of meatballs reads 165°F. Set oven control to broil. Broil with tops of meatballs 4 to 6 inches from heat 2 to 3 minutes or until browned. Remove from oven; cool slightly.

4 Meanwhile, in small bowl, stir together sauce ingredients.

5 To serve, place ½ cup lettuce in each pita half; top with 2 meatballs, ¼ cup yogurt sauce, tomatoes and cilantro.

1 SERVING Calories 210; Total Fat 5g (Saturated Fat 1g, Trans Fat 0g); Cholesterol 35mg; Sodium 430mg; Total Carbohydrate 24g (Dietary Fiber 3g); Protein 18g **CARBOHYDRATE CHOICES:** 1½

Betty's Kitchen Tip Try topping with mango chutney, pomegranate molasses, pomegranate seeds or hummus for extra color and flavor.

Betty's Kitchen Tip To make into kabobs instead, soak 8 (8-inch) bamboo skewers in water 15 minutes. Divide chicken mixture into 8 portions and form into flat log over end of each skewer. Place on pan. Continue as directed in recipe.

Here's a simple dish that's easy enough for a weeknight dinner. Thyme, garlic, honey and lemon transform chicken and broccoli in a fresh new way.

CARB CHOICES

1

Lemon-Garlic Chicken with Broccoli

PREP TIME: 15 Minutes / **START TO FINISH:** 25 Minutes / *4 servings*

BROCCOLI

- 1 teaspoon olive oil
- 2 teaspoons honey
- ⅛ teaspoon salt
- 6 cups broccoli florets, cut into bite-size pieces

CHICKEN

- 1 teaspoon olive oil
- ¼ teaspoon salt
- ¼ teaspoon pepper

- 1 lb uncooked chicken breast tenders (not breaded)
- 2 cloves garlic, finely chopped
- ¼ cup reduced-sodium chicken broth
- 2 tablespoons fresh lemon juice
- 1 tablespoon fresh thyme leaves

1 Move oven racks to upper and lower thirds of oven. Heat oven to 375°F.

2 In large bowl, mix all broccoli ingredients except broccoli until blended. Add broccoli; toss until evenly coated. Place on ungreased 15×10×1-inch pan; place in oven. Immediately reduce heat to 325°F. Bake 20 to 25 minutes or until tender. Remove from oven. Cover to keep warm.

3 Meanwhile, in medium bowl, mix olive oil, salt and pepper. Add chicken; toss to coat.

4 Heat 12-inch ovenproof skillet over medium-high heat. Cook chicken 4 to 5 minutes or until browned on bottom. Turn chicken and top with garlic and chicken broth; transfer to oven. Bake 10 to 15 minutes or until instant-read meat thermometer inserted into thickest part of chicken reads 165°F. Carefully remove pan from oven, being mindful of hot handle.

5 Divide broccoli and chicken among 4 plates. Spoon pan juices and garlic over chicken and broccoli. Drizzle lemon juice on top and sprinkle with thyme.

1 SERVING Calories 230; Total Fat 7g (Saturated Fat 1.5g, Trans Fat 0g); Cholesterol 70mg; Sodium 370mg; Total Carbohydrate 13g (Dietary Fiber 3g); Protein 29g **CARBOHYDRATE CHOICES:** 1

Betty's Kitchen Tip Like it spicy? Add ½ teaspoon sriracha sauce to the broccoli before roasting.

Betty's Kitchen Tip Cutting your own florets from stalks of broccoli? Don't toss out that broccoli stalk! Trim the bottom, peel, then cut into small chunks and roast alongside the florets.

For a delicious accompaniment to this dish, spray skillet with cooking spray; heat over medium-high heat until hot. Add sliced fresh zucchini and onion and cook, stirring occasionally, until crisp-tender. Sprinkle with black pepper and/or crushed red pepper flakes.

Coconut Curry Chicken

PREP TIME: 35 Minutes / **START TO FINISH:** 35 Minutes / *6 servings*

CURRY SAUCE

- ⅔ cup unsweetened coconut milk (from 13.66 oz-can; not cream of coconut)
- ½ cup water
- 2 tablespoons red or green Thai curry paste
- 1 teaspoon packed brown sugar
- 1 teaspoon curry powder
- 1 cup frozen sweet peas (from 12-oz bag)

CHICKEN

- 1¼ lb boneless skinless chicken breasts, cut into 1-inch pieces
- 1 small onion, chopped (½ cup)
- 1 tablespoon canola oil
- 3 cups hot cooked basmati or regular long-grain white rice
- 2 tablespoons chopped dry-roasted peanuts
- Cilantro sprigs

1 In medium bowl, mix all curry sauce ingredients except peas with whisk until smooth. Stir in peas.

2 In 12-inch skillet, heat oil over medium-high heat. Cook chicken and onion in oil 3 to 4 minutes, stirring frequently, or until chicken turns white on outside. Pour curry sauce over chicken. Heat to boiling; reduce heat. Simmer uncovered 10 to 14 minutes, stirring occasionally, or until chicken is no longer pink in center.

3 Serve chicken over rice; garnish with peanuts and cilantro sprigs.

1 SERVING Calories 330; Total Fat 13g (Saturated Fat 6g, Trans Fat 0g); Cholesterol 60mg; Sodium 580mg; Total Carbohydrate 29g (Dietary Fiber 2g); Protein 25g **CARBOHYDRATE CHOICES: 2**

Betty's Kitchen Tip Soy sauce may be substituted for the fish sauce, but the sauce will not have the same depth of flavor.

Make Ahead Mix curry sauce ingredients except peas in 1-gallon resealable freezer plastic bag. Add peas and seal bag. Place chicken and onion in another 1-gallon resealable freezer plastic bag; seal bag. Lay bags flat in freezer. Freeze up to 3 months. Thaw in refrigerator 12 to 24 hours. Continue as directed in step 2.

These lettuce wraps are a perfect summer dinner, or make them ahead on Sunday and enjoy for lunch throughout the week.

CARB CHOICES

1/2

Chicken Salad Lettuce Wraps

PREP TIME: 20 Minutes / **START TO FINISH:** 20 Minutes / *4 wraps*

⅔ cup plain low-fat yogurt

½ teaspoon fresh lime juice

¼ teaspoon salt

¼ teaspoon ground cumin

¼ teaspoon ground coriander

1 cup shredded cooked chicken

4 leaves Bibb lettuce

¾ cup shredded carrot (about 1 large)

¼ cup sliced green onions (4 medium)

¼ cup thinly sliced radishes

¼ cup chopped fresh cilantro

Lime wedges

1 In medium bowl, mix yogurt, lime juice, salt, cumin and coriander. Stir in chicken.

2 To serve, spoon about ¼ cup chicken mixture in center of each lettuce leaf. Top with carrot, onions, radishes and cilantro. Serve with lime wedges.

1 WRAP Calories 100; Total Fat 3.5g (Saturated Fat 1g, Trans Fat 0g); Cholesterol 30mg; Sodium 220mg; Total Carbohydrate 6g (Dietary Fiber 1g); Protein 12g **CARBOHYDRATE CHOICES:** ½

Betty's Kitchen Tip Any cooked chicken (see page 12 or page 17), or even turkey (see page 20), will work well in this recipe.

Betty's Kitchen Tip Bibb lettuce is also sold under the names Boston or butter lettuce. Its tender leaves work great for lettuce wraps.

Make Ahead Prepare the chicken mixture and cut the vegetables; refrigerate separately until serving time. Assemble just before serving.

Spread all of the barbecue sauce on top of the meatloaf, or save some of it to serve with the slices. If you like, cut thin slices of meatloaf so that everyone gets two. Though it's the same amount of meat, this can trick your eye into thinking you are eating more!

CARB CHOICES

1

Turkey-Veggie Meatloaf

PREP TIME: 20 Minutes / **START TO FINISH:** 1 Hour 15 Minutes / *6 servings*

1 lb ground turkey (at least 93% lean)

1 cup chopped fresh baby portabella mushrooms

1 cup shredded zucchini (about 1 small)

¾ cup pure quick-cooking oats

¼ cup finely chopped onion

1½ teaspoons gluten-free Dijon mustard

½ teaspoon salt

½ teaspoon pepper

3 cloves garlic, finely chopped

1 egg

½ cup Strawberry Barbecue Sauce (page 53)

Chopped fresh parsley, if desired

1 Heat oven to 350°F. Spray 8×4-inch loaf pan with cooking spray without flour.

2 In large bowl, gently mix all ingredients except barbecue sauce. Spread mixture in pan.

3 Bake uncovered 40 to 50 minutes or until instant-read meat thermometer inserted in center reads 165°F. Let stand 5 minutes. Using knife, loosen meatloaf around edges of pan; remove from pan to serving platter.

4 In small microwavable bowl, place sauce; cover with plastic wrap. Microwave on High 30 to 60 seconds or until hot; stir. Spoon sauce evenly over top of meatloaf. Sprinkle with parsley.

1 SERVING Calories 210; Total Fat 8g (Saturated Fat 2g, Trans Fat 0g); Cholesterol 90mg; Sodium 340mg; Total Carbohydrate 15g (Dietary Fiber 2g); Protein 18g **CARBOHYDRATE CHOICES:** 1

Betty's Kitchen Tip We suggest using a serrated knife to cut this meatloaf for beautiful, even slices.

Here's a clever way to give frozen meatballs not only new flavor, but also a new use. And best of all, you can do it in the microwave.

CARB CHOICES

1

Turkey Meatball Tacos

PREP TIME: 15 Minutes / **START TO FINISH:** 15 Minutes / *4 tacos*

8 frozen Freezer-Friendly Turkey Meatballs (page 25)
1 tablespoon olive oil
¾ teaspoon ground cumin
¾ teaspoon ground coriander
4 taco shells, heated as directed on package

1 cup shredded lettuce
12 very thin slices jalapeño chile
¼ cup salsa
½ avocado, pitted, peeled and diced
¼ cup crumbled queso fresco cheese (1 oz)
¼ cup chopped fresh cilantro

1 In medium bowl, mix meatballs, oil, cumin and coriander; toss to coat. Place meatballs in single layer on microwavable dish; cover with plastic wrap. Microwave on Medium (50%) 2 to 4 minutes, rotating meatballs halfway through cooking, or until hot (instant-read meat thermometer reads 165°F). Cut meatballs in half.

2 To serve, place ¼ cup lettuce in each taco shell; top each with 4 meatball halves, 3 chile slices, 1 tablespoon salsa, one-quarter of the avocado, and 1 tablespoon each cheese and cilantro.

1 TACO Calories 280; Total Fat 18g (Saturated Fat 4.5g, Trans Fat 0g); Cholesterol 45mg; Sodium 460mg; Total Carbohydrate 16g (Dietary Fiber 2g); Protein 11g **CARBOHYDRATE CHOICES:** 1

When veggies are bountiful, pull some of your frozen cooked turkey or chicken from the freezer for this pretty one-pan weeknight winner.

Turkey-Quinoa Skillet Dinner

PREP TIME: 45 Minutes / **START TO FINISH:** 45 Minutes / *6 servings (about 1 cup each)*

2 tablespoons water

1½ cups 1-inch pieces fresh green beans (6 oz)

1 small yellow summer squash, cut in half lengthwise, then cut crosswise into ¼-inch slices (about 1 cup)

½ cup thinly sliced red onion

1 small red bell pepper, cut into ¼-inch strips (1 cup)

1 teaspoon olive oil

3½ cups gluten-free reduced-sodium chicken broth (for homemade broth, see page 12)

1 cup uncooked quinoa

3 cloves garlic, finely chopped

2 cups cubed Roasted Herbed Turkey Breast (page 20) or cooked chicken or turkey

½ cup sweetened dried cranberries

½ teaspoon salt

¼ teaspoon pepper

¼ cup chopped pecans, toasted

Parsley sprig, if desired

1 In 12-inch nonstick skillet, heat water and green beans over medium-high heat. Cook 2 minutes, stirring occasionally, or until water evaporates. Reduce heat to medium. Add summer squash, onion, bell pepper and oil. Cook uncovered 3 to 5 minutes, stirring occasionally, or until beans are crisp-tender. Remove vegetables from skillet to heatproof plate. Cover to keep warm.

2 In same skillet, add chicken broth, quinoa and garlic. Heat to boiling; reduce heat to low. Cover; cook 13 to 15 minutes, stirring occasionally, or until quinoa is tender and most of the liquid is absorbed. Stir in vegetables, turkey, cranberries, salt and pepper; cook 2 to 3 minutes longer or until thoroughly heated. Sprinkle with pecans and garnish with parsley sprig. Serve immediately.

1 SERVING Calories 320; Total Fat 11g (Saturated Fat 2g, Trans Fat 0g); Cholesterol 35mg; Sodium 410mg; Total Carbohydrate 36g (Dietary Fiber 4g); Protein 20g **CARBOHYDRATE CHOICES:** 2½

Here's where prepping really pays off! This recipe starts with beef from Roast Beef and Vegetables (page 26) to make it easy to get another amazing meal on the table in practically no time.

CARB CHOICES
2½

Roast Beef with Parsnip-Potato Mash and Mushroom Gravy

PREP TIME: 50 Minutes / **START TO FINISH:** 50 Minutes / *4 servings*

PARSNIP-POTATO MASH

- 3 medium parsnips, peeled and chopped (1½ cups)
- 2 medium Yukon Gold potatoes, cubed (2 cups)
- 1 tablespoon butter
- ¼ teaspoon salt
- ¼ teaspoon pepper
- 1 clove garlic, finely chopped

MUSHROOM GRAVY

- 1 teaspoon butter
- 1 package (8 oz) sliced fresh mushrooms (3 cups)
- 1 teaspoon chopped fresh thyme leaves
- ⅛ teaspoon pepper
- 1 tablespoon all-purpose flour
- 1 cup water
- 1 teaspoon low-sodium soy sauce

BEEF AND GARNISH

- 4 servings beef from Roast Beef and Vegetables (page 26)
- 1 tablespoon chopped fresh Italian (flat-leaf) parsley

1 In 3-quart saucepan, place parsnips, potatoes and enough water to just cover them. Heat to boiling; reduce heat. Cover; simmer 18 to 22 minutes or until vegetables are tender when pierced with fork. Drain; return vegetables to pan. Shake pan over low heat to dry vegetables.

2 Add remaining parsnip-potato mash ingredients. Mash in pan with potato masher until fluffy and desired consistency. Cover to keep warm.

3 Spray 10-inch skillet with cooking spray. Add 1 teaspoon butter; heat over medium heat until melted. Stir in mushrooms, thyme and pepper. Cook 5 to 7 minutes, stirring frequently, or until mushrooms are soft and browned. Add flour; stir to coat. Stir water and soy sauce into mushroom mixture. Heat to boiling. Cook uncovered 3 to 5 minutes, stirring occasionally, or until sauce is thickened.

4 Reheat roast beef as directed in Roast Beef and Vegetables recipe. Serve beef with parsnip mash and gravy. Top with parsley.

1 SERVING Calories 350; Total Fat 13g (Saturated Fat 6g, Trans Fat 0.5g); Cholesterol 55mg; Sodium 380mg; Total Carbohydrate 36g (Dietary Fiber 6g); Protein 21g **CARBOHYDRATE CHOICES:** 2½

Here's a clever way to have a burger when living with diabetes. Bulking up very lean ground beef with the hearty flavor and texture of cremini mushrooms and other veggies cooks up a burger you can really sink your teeth into.

Beef-Veggie Burgers with Honey-Horseradish Sauce

PREP TIME: 45 Minutes / **START TO FINISH:** 45 Minutes / *4 servings*

BEEF-VEGGIE PATTIES

- 1 package (8 oz) fresh cremini or whole white mushrooms
- 1 small onion, quartered
- 1 large carrot, peeled if desired
- 1 celery stalk
- 2 teaspoons canola oil
- ½ lb ground beef (at least 96% lean)
- ¾ teaspoon Montreal steak seasoning
- 1 egg white

HONEY-HORSERADISH SAUCE

- 2 tablespoons light mayonnaise
- 2 teaspoons honey
- 1 teaspoon prepared horseradish

BUNS AND TOPPINGS

- 4 leaves lettuce
- 4 tomato slices
- 4 whole wheat hamburger buns (about 4-inch diameter)

1 In food processor fitted with shredding blade or with hand shredder, shred mushrooms, onion, carrot and celery.

2 In 12-inch nonstick skillet, heat 1 teaspoon of the oil over medium heat. Cook and stir vegetables 4 to 5 minutes or until softened. Spoon into fine-mesh strainer. With back of spoon, gently press excess liquid from vegetable mixture; discard liquid. In medium bowl, place vegetables; cool 5 minutes.

3 Add beef, seasoning and egg white; mix well. Shape into 4 patties, each about 3½ inches in diameter.

4 Wipe skillet with paper towel. Heat remaining oil over medium heat. Cook patties 10 to 12 minutes, gently turning once or twice, or until instant-read meat thermometer inserted in center of patties reads 160°F.

5 Meanwhile, in small bowl, mix all sauce ingredients.

6 Place lettuce and tomato on bun bottom; top with patties. Drizzle sauce over patties; cover with bun tops.

1 SERVING Calories 260; Total Fat 8g (Saturated Fat 1.5g, Trans Fat 0g); Cholesterol 40mg; Sodium 470mg; Total Carbohydrate 29g (Dietary Fiber 4g); Protein 19g **CARBOHYDRATE CHOICES:** 2

Coating the pork chops not only adds flavor and texture, but it protects the delicate meat from overcooking and getting tough.

CARB
CHOICES
1

Garlic-Herb Pork Chops

PREP TIME: 20 Minutes / **START TO FINISH:** 20 Minutes / *4 servings*

4 boneless thin cut pork loin chops (about 1 lb total)
1 teaspoon garlic salt
¼ cup all-purpose flour
¾ cup plain panko crispy bread crumbs
1 tablespoon chopped fresh parsley

2 teaspoons chopped fresh basil leaves
2 teaspoons chopped fresh oregano leaves
3 tablespoons milk
2 teaspoons olive or canola oil

1 One at a time, place pork chops between pieces of plastic wrap or waxed paper; gently pound with flat side of meat mallet or rolling pin until about ¼ inch thick. Sprinkle both sides of chops with garlic salt.

2 Place flour in shallow bowl. In another shallow bowl, mix bread crumbs, parsley, basil and oregano. Place milk in separate shallow bowl. Dip each pork chop in flour, then dip in milk. Coat well with bread crumb mixture.

3 In 12-inch nonstick skillet, heat oil over medium heat. Cook pork 7 to 9 minutes, turning once, or until browned and no longer pink in center.

1 SERVING Calories 280; Total Fat 12g (Saturated Fat 3.5g, Trans Fat 0g); Cholesterol 70mg; Sodium 330mg; Total Carbohydrate 16g (Dietary Fiber 0g); Protein 27g **CARBOHYDRATE CHOICES:** 1

When you're craving warm comfort food, this will do the trick. It will feel like eating a decadent casserole—mmm.

Skinny Smothered Pork Chops

PREP TIME: 35 Minutes / **START TO FINISH:** 35 Minutes / *6 servings*

6 boneless pork loin chops (1½ lb total)

1 teaspoon canola oil

1 small onion, chopped (½ cup)

1 package (8 oz) sliced fresh mushrooms (3 cups)

1 can (10¾ oz) condensed 98% fat-free cream of mushroom soup with 45% less sodium

¼ cup water

½ teaspoon reduced-sodium soy sauce

¼ teaspoon dried sage or thyme leaves

⅛ teaspoon pepper

½ cup fat-free sour cream

1 Trim any visible fat from pork chops. Heat 12-inch nonstick skillet over medium-high heat. Add pork; cook about 4 minutes on each side until lightly browned. Remove pork from skillet; set aside.

2 In same skillet, heat oil over medium heat. Add onion and mushrooms; cook 3 minutes, stirring frequently.

3 Stir in soup, water, soy sauce, sage and pepper until well mixed. Heat to boiling. Return pork chops to skillet; spoon sauce over pork. Reduce heat. Cover; simmer 12 to 15 minutes, stirring and turning pork chops occasionally, or until pork is no longer pink in center.

4 Stir in sour cream until well blended and smooth; cook and stir just until hot. Serve pork chops with mushroom sauce.

1 SERVING Calories 240; Total Fat 11g (Saturated Fat 3.5g, Trans Fat 0g); Cholesterol 70mg; Sodium 260mg; Total Carbohydrate 10g (Dietary Fiber 0g); Protein 27g **CARBOHYDRATE CHOICES:** ½

Easy enough for a weeknight yet impressive enough to serve guests. Prepare yourself for the amazing smells coming out of your kitchen when you make this! They're going to make you good and hungry.

CARB CHOICES

0

Spinach and Basil-Stuffed Pork Tenderloin

PREP TIME: 20 Minutes / **START TO FINISH:** 1 Hour / *8 servings*

STUFFING
- 1 tablespoon olive or canola oil
- 1 large clove garlic, finely chopped
- 1 box (9 oz) frozen chopped spinach, thawed, well drained
- ⅓ cup chopped fresh or 4½ teaspoons dried basil leaves
- ¼ teaspoon salt
- ⅛ teaspoon pepper
- 1 egg

PORK TENDERLOIN
- 2 pork tenderloins (1½ lb each), trimmed of visible fat
- 1 tablespoon olive or canola oil
- 1 large clove garlic, finely chopped
- 1 teaspoon fennel seed, crushed

1 Heat oven to 375°F. In 8-inch skillet, heat 1 tablespoon oil over medium-high heat. Add 1 garlic clove; cook and stir 30 to 60 seconds or until garlic is fragrant. Remove from heat. Stir in remaining stuffing ingredients.

2 Butterfly each pork tenderloin by making a horizontal lengthwise cut ¾ of the way through, being careful not to cut tenderloin into two pieces. Open each tenderloin and lay flat.

3 Spread stuffing evenly over cut side of 1 tenderloin. Place second tenderloin, cut side down, over stuffing; to ensure even cooking, place wide end of 1 tenderloin at narrow end of the other. Tie at intervals with kitchen string.

4 In small bowl, mix remaining pork tenderloin ingredients. Brush tenderloin with oil mixture; place on rack in shallow roasting pan.

5 Roast 35 to 45 minutes or until instant-read meat thermometer inserted in center of pork reads 160°F (for medium). Cover loosely with foil; let stand 10 minutes before removing string and cutting into slices.

1 SERVING Calories 270; Total Fat 12g (Saturated Fat 3g, Trans Fat 0g); Cholesterol 125mg; Sodium 180mg; Total Carbohydrate 1g (Dietary Fiber 0g); Protein 40g **CARBOHYDRATE CHOICES:** 0

Betty's Kitchen Tip Crush the fennel seed with a mortar and pestle or place in a small resealable plastic bag and crush with a rolling pin.

The great taste of Buffalo sauce isn't just for chicken wings! Salmon goes zesty and crunchy at the same time with Buffalo-style hot sauce and panko bread crumbs!

CARB CHOICES

1/2

Panko-Crusted Buffalo Salmon

PREP TIME: 5 Minutes / **START TO FINISH:** 20 Minutes / *4 servings*

1 lb skin-on salmon fillet

¼ cup Buffalo-style hot sauce (from 5-oz bottle)

½ cup plain panko crispy bread crumbs

1 Heat oven to 425°F. Line cookie sheet with foil.

2 Place salmon fillet skin side down on cookie sheet. Brush with 2 tablespoons of the hot sauce. Sprinkle with bread crumbs, pressing to coat. Spray lightly with cooking spray.

3 Bake 15 minutes or until crumbs are golden and fish flakes easily with fork. Cut salmon into 4 pieces (should slide off skin). Drizzle with remaining 2 tablespoons hot sauce.

1 SERVING Calories 250; Total Fat 11g (Saturated Fat 2.5g, Trans Fat 0g); Cholesterol 65mg; Sodium 270mg; Total Carbohydrate 10g (Dietary Fiber 0g); Protein 26g **CARBOHYDRATE CHOICES:** ½

Betty's Kitchen Tip Before cooking salmon fillets, run your fingers over the flesh to detect any little bones, and pull them out.

Betty's Kitchen Tip Not all Buffalo sauces are alike. If you're watching sodium, check labels. We used a Buffalo-style hot sauce from a 5-oz bottle, which is lower in sodium than products labeled as Buffalo wing sauce from larger bottles.

EATING OUT

You may think that following a meal plan means you can never eat out in restaurants—not true! You can work restaurant meals into your guidelines with a little planning. Follow these tips to help you stay on track.

Many restaurants offer healthy options; they share not only their menus online, but the nutrition information for their meals as well. When eating out, try to plan ahead, finding a restaurant with food you want to eat as well as what fits into your meal plan.

Before You Go

Here are some tips for choosing restaurants that will have foods you can eat. Scan the menu for these things to know that you'll be able to find suitable dishes. If you're unsure, call the restaurant and ask about:

Preparation Methods Choose dishes that are *grilled, broiled, roasted or steamed.* These preparation methods will generally make dishes lower in fat and calories than other methods.

Whole-Grain and Lower-Fat Ingredients Look for whole-grain breads or rolls, and whole grains such as quinoa, barley or brown rice instead of white rice. Scan the menu for dishes like skinless chicken, and for dishes that can be prepared with less fat, sugar and sodium. Call ahead and ask for these changes to the foods you are interested in . . . many restaurants will be happy to make you happy!

Healthy Options Are there any dishes like grilled veggies, side salads or a fruit cup that you can substitute for higher-carb, high-fat sides like French fries? Look for low-fat or fat-free salad dressing choices.

Making Reservations

Now that you've selected a restaurant, the next important thing is to make reservations. Try to eat about the same time you normally eat. If that isn't an option, or in case your reservation is delayed, be sure to have a small snack with you that you can eat if necessary.

When You Get There

Watch Portion Sizes Some of the appeal of eating out is large restaurant portions—so be mindful of serving sizes. One restaurant chicken breast might be more like two according to your eating plan. Prepare to share the remaining portion, or bring it home for another meal.

Skip Sauces or Get Them on the Side Ask for salad dressings and other sauces on the side, so you can control the amount you eat. An easy way to eat less salad dressing is to dip your fork into the dressing and then into the salad, rather than covering the entire salad with the dressing. Ask for salsa or pico de gallo instead of cheese and sour cream for Mexican-style dishes, and ketchup, mustard, tomato slices or dill pickles instead of mayo-based sauces on burgers.

Be Toppings Selective Keep your eye on salad fixings like croutons, cheese and bacon, which can quickly add calories, carbohydrates and fat. Go for the fresh veggies instead, such as shredded carrots, chopped tomatoes and diced cucumbers.

Choose an Unsweetened Beverage Coffee, tea, water or sparkling water are great choices, as long as they are unsweetened. Talk to your doctor about whether alcohol can be an occasional option for you.

Be Thoughtful About Dessert As long as you plan for the carbs as part of your meal plan, you may be able to eat dessert. Check with your healthcare team to know for sure. Stick to an appropriate portion by sharing the dessert with others. See page 310 for more information about eating dessert.

Using instant brown rice will allow it to be done cooking at the same time as the fish—regular brown rice won't get done quick enough for this recipe.

CARB CHOICES

4

Halibut and Veggie Oven Packets

PREP TIME: 25 Minutes / **START TO FINISH:** 45 Minutes / *2 servings*

- ½ cup water
- ½ cup instant brown rice (from 14-oz box)
- 1 cup chopped bell pepper (any color)
- 1 cup chopped fresh asparagus spears
- 1 teaspoon finely chopped garlic
- ¾ teaspoon chopped fresh rosemary leaves
- ½ teaspoon kosher (coarse) salt
- ¼ teaspoon coarse ground black pepper
- ½ lb halibut fillets (½ to ¾ inch thick)
- ¼ cup dry white wine or gluten-free reduced-sodium chicken broth (for homemade broth, see page 12)
- ½ teaspoon lemon zest

1 Heat oven to 375°F. Cut 2 (18×12-inch) pieces of heavy-duty foil; spray foil with cooking spray.

2 In 1-quart saucepan, heat water to boiling; stir in rice, bell pepper, asparagus and ½ teaspoon of the garlic. Return to boiling; reduce heat to low. Cover; simmer 5 minutes. Remove saucepan from heat; let stand covered 5 minutes or until water is absorbed. Stir in ½ teaspoon of the rosemary, ¼ teaspoon of the salt and ⅛ teaspoon of the pepper.

3 Spoon rice mixture evenly onto center of each foil piece. Cut halibut into 2 pieces. Place fish on rice mixture; drizzle each with 2 tablespoons wine. Sprinkle halibut with remaining garlic, rosemary, salt and pepper.

4 Bring up 2 sides of foil so edges meet. Seal edges, making tight ½-inch fold; fold again, allowing space for heat circulation and expansion. Fold other sides to seal. Place packets on 15×10×1-inch pan.

5 Bake 15 to 20 minutes. Open packets carefully; fish should flake easily with fork and vegetables should be crisp-tender. Reseal packets; let stand 5 minutes. To serve, place packets on heatproof plates; carefully open foil to allow steam to escape. Garnish with lemon zest.

1 SERVING Calories 380; Total Fat 3g (Saturated Fat 0.5g, Trans Fat 0g); Cholesterol 55mg; Sodium 670mg; Total Carbohydrate 58g (Dietary Fiber 6g); Protein 27g **CARBOHYDRATE CHOICES:** 4

Betty's Kitchen Tip Halibut fillets vary in thickness. Be sure to select a fillet that has even thickness for best doneness results.

Betty's Kitchen Tip See what kind of fish is on sale! You can use other fish with a firm texture, such as grouper, pompano or tuna.

Betty's Kitchen Tip Here's a great way to use up an open bottle of wine! Or if you need to open a bottle and don't think you will drink the rest, purchase a small airline-size bottle.

Roasted or steamed asparagus or broccoli with a squeeze of fresh lemon juice would be a delicious way to complete this meal.

CARB CHOICES
1½

Seared Fish with Fresh Tomato Salsa

PREP TIME: 45 Minutes / **START TO FINISH:** 45 Minutes / *4 servings*

POTATOES
- 1 lb fingerling potatoes, cut in half if necessary to make same size
- 1 teaspoon herbes de Provence
- 1 teaspoon olive oil
- ¼ teaspoon salt

SALSA
- 1 cup diced tomato
- 2 tablespoons diced shallot
- 2 tablespoons fresh lemon juice
- ⅛ teaspoon salt
- 2 cloves garlic, finely chopped

FISH
- 4 (4-oz) fillets white fish (such as mahi or cod)
- 2 teaspoons olive oil
- ½ teaspoon herbes de Provence
- ¼ teaspoon salt
- ¼ cup shredded fresh basil leaves

1 Heat oven to 425° F. Line 15×10×1-inch pan with foil.

2 In large bowl, mix all potato ingredients; toss to coat. Spread in single layer on pan. Roast 20 to 25 minutes or until potatoes are tender when pierced with a fork.

3 Meanwhile, in medium bowl, mix all salsa ingredients; set aside.

4 Rub fish with 1 teaspoon of the oil, the herbes de Provence and salt. In 10-inch nonstick skillet, heat remaining 1 teaspoon oil over medium-high heat. Cook fish 4 to 5 minutes; turn and cook 4 to 5 minutes or until fish flakes easily with fork.

5 Divide potatoes and fish among 4 plates. Top each piece of fish with salsa and basil.

1 SERVING Calories 230; Total Fat 4.5g (Saturated Fat 0.5g, Trans Fat 0g); Cholesterol 85mg; Sodium 480mg; Total Carbohydrate 23g (Dietary Fiber 3g); Protein 24g **CARBOHYDRATE CHOICES:** 1½

Betty's Kitchen Tip If subbing a thinner fish like tilapia for the cod or mahi, take care to reduce the cooking time by about half.

Betty's Kitchen Tip If tomatoes are out of season, try substituting 1 cup drained canned diced tomatoes.

If you have the Mediterranean Herb Marinade, you already have a jump-start on this recipe. If you don't, making it will get you one step closer to another meal, since you'll have some leftover to marinate chicken, meat or veggies.

CARB CHOICES
1

Fish-Cauliflower Cakes with Easy Tartar Sauce

PREP TIME: 30 Minutes / **START TO FINISH:** 30 Minutes / *4 servings (3 fish cakes and 2 tablespoon sauce each)*

¾ lb skinless cod, haddock or other medium-firm fish fillets

1½ cups cooked cauliflower florets, well-drained

1¼ cups plain panko crispy bread crumbs

¼ cup chopped green onions (4 medium)

¼ cup Mediterranean Herb Marinade (page 50)

2 egg whites

1 tablespoon canola oil

½ cup light mayonnaise

Dash to ⅛ teaspoon ground red pepper (cayenne)

Additional chopped green onion and lemon wedges, if desired

1 Heat oven to 200°F.

2 In food processor, place fish, cauliflower, ½ cup of the bread crumbs, ⅓ cup onions, 3 tablespoons of the marinade and the egg whites. Cover; process with quick on-and-off pulses 7 to 10 times or until coarsely chopped.

3 Shape into 12 patties each about 2½ inches in diameter, using scant ¼ cup mixture. Coat both sides with remaining bread crumbs.

4 Heat 1½ teaspoons of the oil in 10- or 12-inch skillet over medium heat. Cook 6 patties 10 to 12 minutes, turning halfway through cooking, or until golden brown and instant-read thermometer inserted in center of patties reads 145°F. Remove from pan to heatproof plate or pan. Keep warm in oven. Wipe out skillet with paper towel; repeat with remaining oil and fish cakes.

5 Meanwhile, stir together mayonnaise, red pepper and remaining 1 tablespoon Mediterranean Herb Marinade. Sprinkle fish cakes with additional chopped green onion. Serve sauce and lemon wedges with fish cakes.

1 SERVING Calories 210; Total Fat 10g (Saturated Fat 1g, Trans Fat 0g); Cholesterol 25mg; Sodium 380mg; Total Carbohydrate 16g (Dietary Fiber 1g); Protein 13g **CARBOHYDRATE CHOICES:** 1

Make Ahead Prepare the fish cake mixture and shape as directed in Step 3, but do not coat with panko crumbs. Cover; refrigerate up to 2 hours before cooking. Coat both sides of patties with panko crumbs as directed in Step 3; continue as directed.

Stir-frying is a wonderful, quick-cooking technique that brings out the best in fresh vegetables. Try this dish starring kale, sugar snap peas, carrots and mushrooms.

CARB CHOICES

2

Kale and Tofu Stir-Fry

PREP TIME: 25 Minutes / **START TO FINISH:** 25 Minutes / *4 servings*

- 1 package (14 oz) firm tofu, drained, cut into ¾-inch cubes
- 2 teaspoons canola oil
- 1 clove garlic, finely chopped
- 1 piece (1 inch) gingerroot, grated
- 1 cup fresh sugar snap peas, strings removed
- 1 cup sliced fresh mushrooms (from 8-oz package)

- 1 medium carrot, cut into julienne pieces (1½×¼×¼ inch)
- 1 bunch (8 oz) fresh kale, thick stems removed, leaves cut crosswise into thin strips (6 cups)
- 2 tablespoons gluten-free reduced-sodium soy sauce
- 1 teaspoon sesame oil
- 2 cups hot cooked brown rice

1 Press tofu between paper towels to absorb excess moisture. Set aside. In 12-inch nonstick skillet or large wok, heat canola oil over medium-high heat. Add tofu. Cook 3 to 4 minutes, stirring occasionally, or until light golden brown. Remove tofu from skillet to plate or bowl; cover to keep warm.

2 In same skillet, cook garlic and gingerroot 1 minute, stirring occasionally. Stir in sugar snap peas, mushrooms and carrot. Cook 3 to 5 minutes, stirring constantly, or until mushrooms begin to brown. Add kale; cook about 2 minutes, stirring constantly, or until kale wilts. Stir in tofu, soy sauce and sesame oil until well mixed and heated through. Serve over rice.

1 SERVING Calories 280; Total Fat 9g (Saturated Fat 1.5g, Trans Fat 0g); Cholesterol 0mg; Sodium 720mg; Total Carbohydrate 34g (Dietary Fiber 5g); Protein 15g **CARBOHYDRATE CHOICES:** 2

Betty's Kitchen Tip To save time, cut tofu and prep the vegetables the day ahead; stir-fry when ready to serve.

This delish dish can be on your table in 30 minutes, making it feel (and taste) like good takeout! You can serve it in Chinese paper containers from your local party store and eat it with chopsticks, if you like, for the complete take-out experience.

CARB CHOICES

3

Tofu-Broccoli Stir-Fry

PREP TIME: 30 Minutes / **START TO FINISH:** 30 Minutes / *4 servings (about ¾ cup tofu and ½ cup rice each)*

- 1 package (14 oz) extra-firm tofu, drained, cut into ¾-inch cubes
- 1 cup reduced-sodium vegetable broth (for homemade broth, see page 29)
- 2 tablespoons cornstarch
- 3 tablespoons gluten-free reduced-sodium soy sauce
- 1 teaspoon Asian chili garlic sauce

- 2 tablespoons vegetable oil
- 3 cloves garlic, chopped
- 1 teaspoon grated gingerroot
- 3 cups broccoli florets (7 oz)
- ⅔ cup chopped raw cashews
- 2 cups hot cooked brown rice
- 2 medium green onions, cut diagonally into ½-inch pieces
- 1 teaspoon sesame seed

1 Press tofu cubes between layers of paper towels to remove extra moisture. In small bowl, stir together vegetable broth, cornstarch, soy sauce and chili garlic sauce.

2 In 12-inch nonstick skillet, heat oil over medium-high heat. Cook tofu 4 to 5 minutes or until light brown on one side. Turn tofu pieces; cook 2 to 4 minutes longer, stirring occasionally, or until golden brown on all sides. Add garlic and gingerroot. Cook 30 seconds, stirring constantly.

3 Stir in vegetable broth mixture and broccoli. Heat to boiling; reduce heat to low. Cook 2 to 3 minutes, stirring frequently, or until broccoli is crisp-tender. Remove from heat. Stir in ⅓ cup of the cashews. To serve, top individual servings of stir-fry and rice with remaining ⅓ cup cashews, onions and sesame seed.

1 SERVING Calories 460; Total Fat 23g (Saturated Fat 4g, Trans Fat 0g); Cholesterol 0mg; Sodium 360mg; Total Carbohydrate 44g (Dietary Fiber 4g); Protein 19g **CARBOHYDRATE CHOICES:** 3

Betty's Kitchen Tip Patting the tofu dry will allow it to develop a nice brown color when cooked, while also helping the tofu release from the pan.

A homemade, flavorful crust that's also gluten free—winner, winner pizza dinner! If you like, add thin bell pepper or onion strips or sliced mushrooms before adding the basil and cheeses, for another way to make this pizza delicious.

Fresh Basil and Tomato Pizza

PREP TIME: 15 Minutes / **START TO FINISH:** 2 Hours 5 Minutes / *6 servings*

CRUST

- 1 package fast-acting dry yeast (2¼ teaspoons)
- ⅔ cup warm water (105°F to 115°F)
- 1 tablespoon extra-virgin olive oil
- 1 egg white
- 1¼ cups gluten-free all-purpose rice flour blend
- 1 tablespoon sugar
- 1 teaspoon xanthan gum
- ½ teaspoon salt

TOPPING

- ½ cup canned crushed tomatoes, undrained (from 14- to 15-oz can)
- 1 teaspoon extra-virgin olive oil
- 2 cloves garlic, finely chopped
- ¼ teaspoon salt
- ⅛ teaspoon pepper
- ¼ cup loosely packed fresh basil leaves, cut into thin strips
- ¼ cup finely shredded Parmesan cheese (1 oz)
- 4 oz fresh mozzarella cheese, cut into ¼-inch slices

1 In large bowl, stir together yeast and water; let stand 5 minutes. Stir in 1 tablespoon of the oil and the egg white. Stir in flour blend, sugar, xanthan gum and ½ teaspoon of the salt. Cover with plastic wrap. Let stand in warm place 1 hour.

2 Spray 12-inch pizza pan or large cookie sheet with cooking spray. Place dough on pan. Press into 11-inch circle. Cover; let rise 30 minutes. Meanwhile, heat oven to 425°F.

3 With wet fingers, press dough into 12-inch circle. Bake 10 to 12 minutes or until edges begin to brown. Remove pan from oven. Increase oven temperature to 450°F.

4 In small bowl, stir together tomatoes, oil, garlic, salt and pepper. Spread evenly over crust to within ½ inch of edge. Sprinkle with basil and Parmesan cheese. Arrange mozzarella cheese evenly over toppings. Bake about 8 minutes longer or until cheese is bubbly and edge is golden brown. Let stand 1 to 2 minutes before slicing.

1 SERVING Calories 220; Total Fat 9g (Saturated Fat 4g, Trans Fat 0g); Cholesterol 20mg; Sodium 490mg; Total Carbohydrate 25g (Dietary Fiber 1g); Protein 8g **CARBOHYDRATE CHOICES:** 1½

An easy fix-and-forget lasagna that can be made hours before you need it. The fresh veggies add delicious flavor and color to a family favorite.

Spinach Lasagna

PREP TIME: 30 Minutes / **START TO FINISH:** 4 Hours 40 Minutes / *8 servings*

- 1 jar (25.5 oz) tomato basil pasta sauce
- 1 can (14.5 oz) fire-roasted crushed or diced tomatoes, undrained
- ¼ teaspoon crushed red pepper flakes
- 1 yellow bell pepper, seeded, coarsely chopped
- 1 small zucchini, cut in half lengthwise, then cut crosswise into ¼-inch slices

- 9 uncooked lasagna noodles
- 1¼ cups light ricotta cheese
- 1½ cups shredded part-skim mozzarella cheese (6 oz)
- 4 cups coarsely chopped fresh baby spinach leaves (4 oz)

1 Spray 5- to 6-quart slow cooker with cooking spray. In medium bowl, mix pasta sauce, tomatoes, red pepper flakes, bell pepper and zucchini. Spread 1 cup of the tomato mixture in bottom of slow cooker.

2 Place 3 lasagna noodles, broken into pieces to fit if necessary, on top of sauce in slow cooker. Spread half of the ricotta cheese over noodles; sprinkle with ¼ cup of the mozzarella cheese and half of the spinach. Top with one-third of the remaining tomato sauce mixture (about 1½ cups). Repeat layering of noodles, cheeses and spinach. Top with remaining 3 noodles and sauce. Reserve remaining 1 cup mozzarella cheese in refrigerator.

3 Cover; cook on Low heat setting 4 to 5 hours or until noodles are tender and cooked through. Sprinkle with reserved mozzarella cheese; re-cover and let stand 10 minutes to melt cheese.

1 SERVING Calories 290; Total Fat 11g (Saturated Fat 5g, Trans Fat 0g); Cholesterol 25mg; Sodium 480mg; Total Carbohydrate 32g (Dietary Fiber 4g); Protein 15g **CARBOHYDRATE CHOICES:** 2

Make It Your Own Try up to 2 cups other vegetables in the lasagna, such as sliced mushrooms, sliced yellow summer squash, thinly sliced red onion, grated carrots or green bell pepper, instead of the yellow bell pepper and zucchini.

High-protein spaghetti and edamame lend protein to this pasta dish, making it a delicious and colorful meatless meal. Look for high-protein pasta near the other dried pastas in your supermarket.

Thai-Style Noodles and Veggies

PREP TIME: 30 Minutes / **START TO FINISH:** 30 Minutes / *6 servings (1½ cups each)*

6 oz protein-added spaghetti

2 teaspoons vegetable oil

2 cups shredded red cabbage

1½ cups frozen shelled edamame, thawed

1¼ cups shredded carrots (about 1½ medium)

1¼ cups red bell pepper strips (1×¼-inch)

1¼ cups yellow bell pepper (1×¼-inch)

¼ cup sliced green onions (4 medium)

¾ cup Thai Peanut-Coconut Sauce (page 48)

2 teaspoons sesame seed

Basil leaves

1 In 5-quart Dutch oven, cook and drain spaghetti as directed on package. Return spaghetti to Dutch oven; cover to keep warm.

2 Meanwhile, in 12-inch nonstick skillet, heat oil over medium-high heat. Add red cabbage, edamame, carrots, peppers, and onions. Cook 4 to 6 minutes uncovered, stirring frequently, or until vegetables are crisp-tender. Remove from heat; stir in peanut-coconut sauce.

3 Add vegetable mixture to hot cooked spaghetti; toss gently to coat. Sprinkle with sesame seed and garnish with basil leaves. Serve immediately.

1 SERVING Calories 290; Total Fat 10g (Saturated Fat 1.5g, Trans Fat 0g); Cholesterol 0mg; Sodium 280mg; Total Carbohydrate 35g (Dietary Fiber 7g); Protein 15g **CARBOHYDRATE CHOICES:** 2

Betty's Kitchen Tip Garnish with this creamy noodle dish with either Thai basil or regular basil leaves. Not only does it enhance the presentation, but you can cut up the leaves to enjoy with the dish, as the aroma and flavor go well with the dish.

Roasted cauliflower and crunchy seasoned chick peas make a refreshing and tasty change of pace for tacos, especially if you're only used to eating them filled with meat. The cilantro-pepita pesto knocks it out of the park.

CARB CHOICES 1½

Chick Pea and Cauliflower Tacos

PREP TIME: 30 Minutes / **START TO FINISH:** 40 Minutes / *8 tacos*

ROASTED CAULIFLOWER

- 1 medium head cauliflower (2 lb), separated into florets
- 2 tablespoons olive oil
- ¼ teaspoon salt

CRISPY CHICK PEAS

- 1 can (15 oz) chick peas (garbanzo beans), rinsed, drained
- 1 tablespoon olive oil
- ⅛ teaspoon salt
- ¼ teaspoon chili powder
- ¼ teaspoon ground cumin
- ¼ teaspoon ground oregano

CILANTRO-PEPITA PESTO

- 2 cups lightly packed fresh cilantro leaves
- ⅓ cup hulled pumpkin seeds (pepitas)
- 2 tablespoons chopped, seeded jalapeño chiles
- 2 tablespoons fresh lime juice
- ⅛ teaspoon salt
- 1 small clove garlic, cut in half
- 2 tablespoons olive oil
- 2 tablespoons water

TORTILLAS

- 8 gluten-free white corn tortillas

1 Heat oven to 425°F. In large bowl, stir together all cauliflower ingredients until evenly coated. Arrange on ungreased large cookie sheet. Bake 15 minutes; stir. Bake 15 to 20 minutes longer or until cauliflower is tender and browned.

2 Meanwhile, in small bowl, stir together all chick pea ingredients. Spread on ungreased 15×10×1-inch pan. Bake 15 minutes; stir. Bake 10 to 15 minutes longer or until chickpeas are slightly browned and crispy.

3 Meanwhile, in food processor, place all pesto ingredients except oil and water. Cover; process using quick on-and-off pulses, until finely chopped. With food processor running, slowly drizzle oil and water through feed tube, stopping occasionally to scrape down side with rubber spatula, until smooth. Remove pesto to small bowl.

4 Heat tortillas as directed on package. Spoon about 1 tablespoon pesto onto each tortilla. Top with about ½ cup roasted cauliflower and 1 tablespoon chick peas. Serve with remaining chick peas on the side.

2 TACOS Calories 230; Total Fat 13g (Saturated Fat 2g, Trans Fat 0g); Cholesterol 0mg; Sodium 270mg; Total Carbohydrate 23g (Dietary Fiber 5g); Protein 6g **CARBOHYDRATE CHOICES:** 1½

Betty's Kitchen Tip Garnish tacos with whole or chopped cilantro leaves.

Here's a meatless beans-and-greens recipe that can be on the table in less than 30 minutes. The comforting homemade flavors will satisfy your craving for a hearty, warm one-pot dinner.

CARB CHOICES

3

Beans with Spinach and Mushrooms

PREP TIME: 15 Minutes / **START TO FINISH:** 25 Minutes / *4 servings (1¾ cups each)*

- 1 tablespoon olive oil
- 1 package (8 oz) sliced fresh mushrooms (3 cups)
- 1 small onion, chopped (½ cup)
- 2 cloves garlic, finely chopped
- ¾ teaspoon dried oregano leaves
- ½ cup reduced-sodium vegetable broth (for homemade broth, see page 29)
- 1 tablespoon cornstarch
- 1 can (15.8 oz) reduced-sodium great northern beans, rinsed, drained

- 1 can (15.5 oz) reduced-sodium chick peas (garbanzo beans), rinsed, drained
- 1 can (14.5 oz) diced tomatoes with basil, garlic and oregano, undrained
- 4 cups coarsely chopped fresh spinach or baby spinach leaves (about 5 oz)
- ¼ cup shredded Parmesan cheese (1 oz)

1 Spray 12-inch skillet with cooking spray. Heat oil in skillet over medium-high heat. Add mushrooms, onion, garlic and oregano. Cook 3 to 5 minutes, stirring frequently, or until mushrooms are tender.

2 In small bowl, stir together vegetable broth and cornstarch.

3 Stir beans, chick peas, tomatoes and vegetable broth mixture into mushrooms in skillet. Heat to boiling; cook 1 minute or until mixture is thickened and bubbly. Gradually stir in spinach. Cook 1 to 2 minutes or until wilted. Sprinkle with cheese.

1 SERVING Calories 340; Total Fat 8g (Saturated Fat 2g, Trans Fat 0g); Cholesterol 0mg; Sodium 290mg; Total Carbohydrate 48g (Dietary Fiber 12g); Protein 18g **CARBOHYDRATE CHOICES:** 3

Betty's Kitchen Tip If you like, you can substitute baby kale or chopped turnip, mustard or beet greens for the spinach leaves. You may need to them cook a minute or two longer for them to wilt.

Stuffed baked potatoes get a makeover, starting with sweet potatoes. Topped with jerk-seasoned pork, a colorful mango salsa and queso fresco, you'll feel like you're taking a trip to the islands.

CARB CHOICES

3½

Tropical Pork-Stuffed Sweet Potatoes

PREP TIME: 20 Minutes / **START TO FINISH:** 1 Hour 45 Minutes / *4 servings*

SWEET POTATOES

- 4 large dark-orange sweet potatoes
- ¼ teaspoon salt

MANGO SALSA

- 1 tablespoon packed brown sugar
- 1 tablespoon fresh lime juice
- 2 teaspoons finely chopped gingerroot
- 1 cup diced mango
- ¼ cup diced red onion
- 1 tablespoon finely chopped seeded jalapeño chile
- 2 tablespoons chopped fresh cilantro

TOPPINGS

- 2 cups frozen Make-Ahead Oven-Roasted Pulled Pork (page 33), thawed
- 1 tablespoon olive oil
- 1½ teaspoons jerk seasoning
- ¼ cup crumbled queso fresco cheese (1 oz)

1 Heat oven to 400°F. Line 15×10×1-inch pan with foil; spray foil with cooking spray. Poke sweet potatoes all over with fork; place on pan.

2 Bake 1 hour to 1 hour 15 minutes or until tender when pierced with a fork. Cool about 10 minutes or until easy to handle.

3 Meanwhile, in small bowl, stir together brown sugar, lime juice, and gingerroot until sugar is dissolved. Add mango, onion and chile; toss to coat. Stir in cilantro. Cover; refrigerate until serving time.

4 In medium microwavable bowl, mix pork, oil and jerk seasoning. Microwave uncovered on High 1 to 2 minutes or until hot.

5 Cut open sweet potatoes; using fork, mash potato flesh. Sprinkle salt over potato; stir in with fork. Top each potato with ½ cup pork mixture, ¼ cup mango salsa and 1 tablespoon cheese.

1 SERVING Calories 510; Total Fat 20g (Saturated Fat 6g, Trans Fat 0g); Cholesterol 75mg; Sodium 630mg; Total Carbohydrate 54g (Dietary Fiber 7g); Protein 28g **CARBOHYDRATE CHOICES:** 3½

Peanut butter and peanut butter chips make these cookies enjoyable to sink your teeth into. Behind the decadent look and texture lies the perfect combination of white whole wheat flour, fat-free egg product and reduced-fat peanut butter, balanced with the other ingredients for a cookie that tastes like it came from a bakery.

CARB CHOICES

1½

Peanut Butter Chip Cookies

PREP TIME: 15 Minutes / **START TO FINISH:** 45 Minutes / *About 2 dozen cookies*

1 cup packed brown sugar

½ cup reduced-fat creamy peanut butter

½ cup butter, softened

¼ cup fat-free egg product

1¼ cups white whole wheat flour

¾ teaspoon baking soda

½ teaspoon baking powder

¼ teaspoon salt

1 cup peanut butter chips (6 oz)

2 tablespoons granulated sugar

1 Heat oven to 375°F.

2 In large bowl, beat brown sugar, peanut butter, butter and egg product with electric mixer on medium speed until creamy. On low speed, beat in flour, baking soda, baking powder and salt. Stir in peanut butter chips.

3 Shape dough into 1½-inch balls. Coat balls with granulated sugar. Onto ungreased cookie sheet, place half of balls about 2 inches apart (do not flatten).

4 Bake 9 to 12 minutes or until light brown. Cool 5 minutes; remove from cookie sheet to cooling rack. Repeat with remaining dough. To store, cool completely and store in tightly covered container.

1 COOKIE Calories 170; Total Fat 8g (Saturated Fat 3g, Trans Fat 0g); Cholesterol 10mg; Sodium 160mg; Total Carbohydrate 21g (Dietary Fiber 1g); Protein 3g **CARBOHYDRATE CHOICES:** 1½

We're warning you now: The combination of fresh orange and ginger scents will fill your kitchen as you bake these delicious cookies. They just beg to be dunked into a cup of hot ginger tea.

Orange-Ginger Biscotti

PREP TIME: 35 Minutes / **START TO FINISH:** 2 Hours / *40 cookies*

⅔ cup granulated sugar

¼ cup butter, melted and cooled

3 tablespoons finely chopped gingerroot

2 tablespoons orange zest

1 teaspoon vanilla

3 eggs

2 cups white whole wheat flour

¾ cup almond flour

1 teaspoon baking powder

¼ teaspoon baking soda

⅛ teaspoon salt

⅓ cup toasted sliced almonds

2 teaspoons powdered sugar

1 Heat oven to 350°F. Spray large cookie sheet with cooking spray.

2 In large bowl, beat granulated sugar, butter, gingerroot, orange zest, vanilla and eggs with electric mixer on medium speed for 2 minutes. Add remaining ingredients except almonds and powdered sugar; mix on low speed until soft dough forms. Stir in almonds; mix well.

3 Divide dough in half (dough will be slightly sticky). On cookie sheet, shape each half into 10×3-inch rectangle, rounding edges slightly, about 3 inches apart.

4 Bake 18 to 22 minutes or until edges are golden brown. Cool on cookie sheet 15 minutes; move to cutting board. Using serrated knife, cut each rectangle crosswise into ½-inch slices.

5 Place slices cut side down on 2 large cookie sheets. Bake 1 cookie sheet about 15 minutes, turning cookies once, or until golden brown. Immediately remove from cookie sheet to cooling rack. Repeat with remaining cookie sheet. Cool completely, about 15 minutes. Sprinkle biscotti lightly with powdered sugar before serving.

1 COOKIE Calories 70; Total Fat 3g (Saturated Fat 1g, Trans Fat 0g); Cholesterol 15mg; Sodium 40mg; Total Carbohydrate 9g (Dietary Fiber 1g); Protein 2g **CARBOHYDRATE CHOICES:** ½

Betty's Kitchen Tip The biscotti will continue to crisp as they cool. To keep them crisp, store the cookies in a loosely covered container.

The comfort of a homemade oatmeal cookie with the decadence of chocolate is an unbeatable combination. Because they spread as they bake, you get a thin but large cookie—what a treat!

CARB CHOICES

1

Chocolate-Drizzled Oatmeal Lace Cookies

PREP TIME: 35 Minutes / **START TO FINISH:** 2 Hours 30 Minutes / *2½ dozen cookies*

½ cup butter, cut into 1-inch pieces

1 cup packed brown sugar

1½ cups old-fashioned oats

¼ cup sliced almonds, chopped

¼ cup all-purpose flour

1½ teaspoons vanilla

¼ teaspoon salt

1 egg white, slightly beaten

¼ cup semisweet chocolate chips

1 Heat oven to 350°F. Line two cookie sheets with cooking parchment paper.

2 In 1-quart saucepan, heat butter and brown sugar over medium-low heat 3 to 5 minutes, stirring constantly, or until butter is melted and mixture can be stirred smooth.

3 Transfer mixture to medium bowl. Stir in oats, almonds, flour, vanilla and salt. Cool 5 minutes; stir in egg white until well mixed.

4 Onto cookie sheet, drop mixture by level tablespoonfuls about 2½ inches apart. Spray back of clean spoon with cooking spray; press each mound with back of spoon to spread into 2½-inch circle, respraying spoon as necessary to prevent sticking.

5 Bake 9 to 11 minutes or until deep golden brown and crisp around edges. Cool until firm, about 3 minutes. With thin metal spatula, carefully remove from cookie sheet to cooling rack. Repeat with remaining dough. Cool completely.

6 In small microwavable bowl, microwave chocolate chips uncovered on High 45 to 60 seconds, stirring every 15 seconds, until melted and can be stirred smooth. Spoon chocolate into small resealable food-storage plastic bag; seal bag. Cut off tiny corner of bag; squeeze bag to drizzle chocolate over each cookie. Cool about 1 hour or until chocolate is set. Store covered in airtight container.

1 COOKIE Calories 90; Total Fat 4g (Saturated Fat 2.5g, Trans Fat 0g); Cholesterol 10mg; Sodium 50mg; Total Carbohydrate 12g (Dietary Fiber 0g); Protein 1g **CARBOHYDRATE CHOICES: 1**

Betty's Kitchen Tip Spraying the back of your spoon before pressing cookies helps avoid sticking.

White Chocolate–Drizzled Oatmeal Lace Cookies For a white drizzle, place ¼ cup white vanilla baking chips in small microwavable bowl and microwave uncovered on Medium (50%) 30 to 60 seconds, stirring after 30 seconds. Continue microwaving in 15-second increments until chips can be stirred smooth. Spoon chocolate into small resealable food-storage plastic bag; seal bag. Cut off tiny corner of bag; squeeze bag to drizzle chocolate over each cookie. Cool until topping is set, about 1 hour.

Here's a big-batch recipe perfect for a crowd or holiday cookie tray. It's also a great recipe to make once to have fresh cookies in minutes—freeze either the baked cookies or the unbaked dough.

CARB CHOICES

1/2

Almond Butter Blossoms

PREP TIME: 35 Minutes / **START TO FINISH:** 3 Hours 20 Minutes / *5 dozen cookies*

½ cup creamy almond butter	½ teaspoon baking powder
½ cup butter, softened	¼ teaspoon salt
½ cup granulated sugar	2 egg whites
½ cup packed brown sugar	1½ cups whole almonds, chopped
1 egg	60 milk chocolate candy drops or pieces, unwrapped (from 10.8-oz bag)
1½ cups all-purpose flour	
¾ teaspoon baking soda	

1 Heat oven to 375°F.

2 In large bowl, beat almond butter, butter, granulated sugar, brown sugar and egg with electric mixer on medium speed or mix with spoon until well blended. Stir in flour, baking soda, baking powder and salt until dough forms.

3 Shape dough into 1-inch balls. In small bowl, beat egg whites lightly with fork. Place chopped almonds in another small bowl. Dip each ball into egg white, then roll in almonds. Onto ungreased cookie sheet, place balls 2 inches apart.

4 Bake 8 to 10 minutes or until edges are light golden brown. Cool 1 minute; press 1 milk chocolate candy into center of each cookie. Remove from cookie sheet to cooling rack. Repeat with remaining dough. To store, cool completely, about 2 hours or until chocolate candy is set. Store in airtight container at room temperature with waxed paper between layers.

1 COOKIE Calories 100; Total Fat 6g (Saturated Fat 2g, Trans Fat 0g); Cholesterol 10mg; Sodium 55mg; Total Carbohydrate 10g (Dietary Fiber 1g); Protein 2g **CARBOHYDRATE CHOICES:** ½

Betty's Kitchen Tip Some almond butters, like peanut butters, have more texture, and some are smoother and creamier. We used creamy, no-stir almond butter for this recipe.

Betty's Kitchen Tip Use a 1-inch cookie or ice cream scoop to make consistently even-shaped cookies.

Betty's Kitchen Tip We like to use chopped whole almonds with skin on to give an attractive look to the cookies. If you prefer a coarser chopped look, chop the almonds by hand. Use a food processor for a more finely chopped look.

Make Ahead **Baked Cookies:** Freeze cooled baked cookies uncovered on cookie sheet 1 to 2 hours or until frozen. Transfer to resealable freezer plastic bag or freezer-safe food storage container; seal bag or tightly cover container. Freeze up to 12 months. To thaw, place as many cookies as desired on plate and let stand at room temperature until thawed, about 30 minutes. **Unbaked Dough:** Prepare dough through Step 3. Freeze balls uncovered on cookie sheet, 1 to 2 hours, or until frozen; transfer to resealable freezer plastic bag. Thaw the desired number of dough balls on a cookie sheet at room temperature, about 30 minutes; continue as directed in Step 4.

Scotcheroos made with whole grains—equally as fun to eat as to say! If you like, sprinkle a few additional puffed quinoa kernels over the frosting before it sets up.

CARB CHOICES

1

Crispy Brown Rice and Quinoa Scotcheroos

PREP TIME: 15 Minutes / **START TO FINISH:** 55 Minutes / *16 bars*

2 cups crispy brown rice cereal

1½ cups puffed quinoa

½ cup reduced-fat vegan peanut butter

¾ cup no-sugar added, stevia-sweetened vegan butterscotch flavor baking chips

¼ cup vegan dark chocolate chips

1 Line 8-inch square pan with foil; set aside.

2 In medium bowl, mix brown rice cereal and quinoa. In small microwavable bowl, mix peanut butter and ½ cup of the butterscotch chips. Microwave uncovered on High 30 seconds; stir. If necessary, continue microwaving on High 15 seconds longer or until melted and can be stirred smooth. Pour over cereal mixture in bowl; stir gently until evenly coated. Press firmly into pan.

3 In small microwavable bowl, microwave remaining ¼ cup butterscotch chips and chocolate chips uncovered on High about 1 minute, stirring every 15 seconds, until melted and smooth. Spread evenly over bars. Refrigerate until firm, about 45 minutes.

4 Cut into 4 rows by 4 rows. Store in tightly covered container in refrigerator.

1 BAR Calories 150; Total Fat 8g (Saturated Fat 3g, Trans Fat 0g); Cholesterol 0mg; Sodium 40mg; Total Carbohydrate 17g (Dietary Fiber 3g); Protein 3g **CARBOHYDRATE CHOICES: 1**

Freeze-dried raspberries work well in this recipe because they add intense flavor without extra liquid. Their dryness makes it easy to process them into a powder. To prevent clumping, be sure your hands are dry before sprinkling them over the meringues.

Raspberry-Chocolate Chip Meringues

PREP TIME: 45 Minutes / **START TO FINISH:** 5 Hours 45 Minutes / *5 dozen cookies*

1 package (1.25 oz) freeze-dried raspberries

4 egg whites, room temperature

¼ teaspoon cream of tartar

½ teaspoon gluten-free vanilla

1 cup sugar

⅛ teaspoon liquid red food color

1 cup miniature semisweet chocolate chips

1½ cups dark chocolate chips (9 oz)

5 teaspoons vegetable shortening

1 Move oven racks to upper and lower thirds of oven. Heat oven to 250°F. Line 2 large cookie sheets with cooking parchment paper.

2 In food processor, place raspberries. Cover; process until finely ground. Reserve 1 teaspoon for decoration.

3 In large bowl, beat egg whites, cream of tartar and vanilla with electric mixer on high speed until foamy. Beat in sugar 1 tablespoon at a time; continue beating until stiff, glossy peaks form and sugar is almost dissolved, 5 to 8 minutes, scraping side of bowl occasionally. Do not underbeat. Add remaining ground raspberries and food color; beat on high speed to blend. Fold miniature chocolate chips into mixture.

4 Fit large decorating bag with large round piping tip. Spoon half of the mixture into bag. Pipe mounds 1½-inches high with 1½-inch base (release squeezing pressure on bag to form tips), 1 inch apart on cookie sheet. Repeat filling decorating bag and piping with remaining meringue mixture.

5 Place cookie sheets in oven on separate racks. Bake 15 minutes. Rotate cookie sheets between racks and from front to back. Bake 15 minutes longer. Turn off oven; leave meringues in oven with door closed 30 minutes.

6 Remove from oven. Sprinkle remaining 1 teaspoon ground raspberries over tops of meringues. Place pans on cooling racks; continue to cool at room temperature, about 2 hours. Remove meringues from parchment paper to cookie sheets lined with clean cooking parchment paper.

7 In small microwavable bowl, microwave dark chocolate chips and shortening uncovered on High 60 seconds; stir. Continue to microwave 30 to 60 seconds, stirring every 15 seconds, until chips can be stirred smooth. Working with one meringue at a time, dip bottom into melted chocolate. Slide bottom of meringue across edge of bowl to remove excess. Return to lined cookie sheet. Repeat with remaining meringues. Let stand about 3 hours or until chocolate is set. Store covered in airtight container in single layer.

1 COOKIE Calories 50; Total Fat 2g (Saturated Fat 1g, Trans Fat 0g); Cholesterol 0mg; Sodium 0mg; Total Carbohydrate 8g (Dietary Fiber 0g); Protein 0g **CARBOHYDRATE CHOICES:** ½

Betty's Kitchen Tip Make sure egg whites are yolk free, or your meringue may deflate. To prevent mixing yolk into the whites, crack eggs one at a time, and place each egg white into a custard cup to ensure it is free of yolk before transferring it to the mixing bowl. A clean glass, metal or copper bowl is best for whipping meringue. Egg whites whip best at room temperature. But for food safety reasons, don't allow eggs to remain at room temperature for more than 30 minutes.

Egg whites whip best at room temperature; for food safety reasons, limit them to 30 minutes at room temperature.

Hot Cocoa Meringues

PREP TIME: 25 Minutes / **START TO FINISH:** 5 Hours 25 Minutes / *3 dozen cookies*

- 4 egg whites, room temperature
- ¼ teaspoon cream of tartar
- ½ teaspoon pure vanilla
- 1 cup sugar
- 2 tablespoons unsweetened dark baking cocoa
- ½ cup dark chocolate chips
- 3 tablespoons gluten-free vegan vanilla marshmallow bits

1 Heat oven to 275°F. Move oven racks to upper and lower thirds of oven. Line 2 large cookie sheets with cooking parchment paper.

2 In large bowl, beat egg whites, cream of tartar and vanilla with electric mixer on high speed until foamy. Beat in sugar 1 tablespoon at a time; continue beating until stiff, glossy peaks form and sugar is almost dissolved, 5 to 6 minutes, scraping side of bowl occasionally. Do not underbeat.

3 In small bowl, place 2 cups of the meringue. Sprinkle cocoa through fine-mesh strainer over top; fold cocoa into meringue. Place large decorating bag fitted with large star piping tip on its side. Using large icing spatula, transfer half of white meringue so it covers one half of the length of inside of piping bag. Carefully spoon half of the cocoa meringue on top of white meringue in bag. Onto cookie sheet, pipe into 2-inch circles. Wash and dry reusable bag (or discard disposable bag). Repeat filling decorating bag with remaining meringues; pipe circles onto second cookie sheet.

4 Place cookie sheets in oven on separate racks. Bake 30 minutes. Turn off oven; leave meringues in oven with door closed 1 hour. Remove from oven, and place pans on cooling racks; continue to cool at room temperature, about 2 hours. Remove from parchment paper; place on cooling racks.

5 Place waxed paper or cooking parchment paper under cooling racks. In small microwavable bowl, microwave chocolate chips uncovered on High 30 to 60 seconds, stirring every 15 seconds, until chips can be stirred smooth. Spoon chocolate into small resealable food-storage plastic bag; seal bag. Cut off tiny corner of bag; squeeze bag to drizzle chocolate over tops of cookies. Sprinkle marshmallow bits over chocolate. Let stand 1 hour 30 minutes or until chocolate is set. Store covered in airtight container in single layer.

1 COOKIE Calories 40; Total Fat 1g (Saturated Fat 0g, Trans Fat 0g); Cholesterol 0mg; Sodium 5mg; Total Carbohydrate 7g (Dietary Fiber 0g); Protein 0g **CARBOHYDRATE CHOICES:** ½

Betty's Kitchen Tip Make sure egg whites are yolk free, or your meringue may deflate. To prevent mixing yolk into the whites, crack eggs one at a time, and place each white into a custard cup to ensure it is free of yolk before transferring it to the mixing bowl. A clean glass, metal or copper bowl is best for whipping meringue.

Betty's Kitchen Tip Vegan marshmallow bits can be found in the baking aisle or the ice cream toppings section of some grocery stores.

This no-sugar-added cake gets its sweetness solely from dates and bananas. The spice combination and the pecan-oat topping turn this snack cake into a delightful treat.

CARB CHOICES

1½

Banana-Cardamom Snack Cake

PREP TIME: 15 Minutes / **START TO FINISH:** 50 Minutes / *9 servings*

⅓ cup chopped pitted dates

3 tablespoons canola oil

½ cup fat-free (skim) milk

1 teaspoon vanilla

1 ripe medium banana

1 egg

1¼ cups whole wheat flour

2 teaspoons baking powder

¾ teaspoon ground cardamom

½ teaspoon ground cinnamon

¼ teaspoon ground nutmeg

¼ teaspoon salt

2 tablespoons chopped pecans

1 tablespoon quick or old-fashioned oats

1 Heat oven to 350°F. Spray 8-inch square baking pan with cooking spray.

2 In food processor, place dates and oil. Cover; process 30 seconds, scraping bowl once or twice, until almost smooth. Add milk, vanilla, banana and egg. Cover; process using quick on-and-off pulses 10 to 15 times until blended. In medium bowl, stir together banana mixture and remaining ingredients except pecans and oatmeal. Spoon into pan. Sprinkle with pecans and oats.

3 Bake 17 to 20 minutes or until toothpick inserted in center comes out clean. Cool in pan on cooling rack 15 minutes. Serve warm or cool.

1 SERVING Calories 170; Total Fat 7g (Saturated Fat 0.5g, Trans Fat 0g); Cholesterol 20mg; Sodium 190mg; Total Carbohydrate 22g (Dietary Fiber 3g); Protein 4g **CARBOHYDRATE CHOICES:** 1½

For an extra burst of lemony lusciousness, sprinkle the cakes with lemon zest after the powdered sugar. It's easy to sprinkle if you zest the lemon while the cakes are baking and cooling, so the zest has time to dry. As it dries, you can rub it between your fingers to separate the pieces.

CARB CHOICES 1/2

Mini Lemon Pound Cakes

PREP TIME: 25 Minutes / **START TO FINISH:** 2 Hours / *5 dozen cakes*

¾ cup butter, softened

4 oz (half of 8-oz package) cream cheese, softened

1½ cups granulated sugar

3 eggs

1½ cups all-purpose flour

⅛ teaspoon salt

2 teaspoons lemon zest

2 tablespoons fresh lemon juice

¼ cup powdered sugar

1 Heat oven to 350°F. Place mini paper baking cup in each of 24 mini muffin cups; spray paper cups with cooking spray.

2 In large bowl, beat butter and cream cheese with electric mixer on medium speed 2 minutes or until light and fluffy. Gradually add granulated sugar, beating until blended. Beat on medium speed 5 minutes. Add eggs, one at a time; beat just until blended after each addition. On low speed, beat in flour and salt until smooth. Beat in lemon zest and juice. Fill muffin cups two-thirds full. (Cover and refrigerate remaining batter until ready to bake; cool pan 15 minutes before reusing.)

3 Bake 15 to 17 minutes or until toothpick inserted in center comes out clean. Cool 10 minutes; remove from pans to cooling racks. Repeat with remaining batter to make an additional 36 mini cakes. Cool completely. Sprinkle cakes with powdered sugar before serving.

1 CAKE Calories 60; Total Fat 3g (Saturated Fat 2g, Trans Fat 0g); Cholesterol 0mg; Sodium 35mg; Total Carbohydrate 8g (Dietary Fiber 0g); Protein 0g **CARBOHYDRATE CHOICES:** ½

Pumpkin and fat-free Greek yogurt add to the moistness of this cake, without your even knowing they are there. It was a hit at taste panels, so the title is a perfect description of what you get!

Delicious Chocolate Cake

PREP TIME: 15 Minutes / **START TO FINISH:** 1 Hour 5 Minutes / *10 servings*

- 1 cup whole wheat flour
- 1½ teaspoons baking powder
- ½ teaspoon baking soda
- 2 oz unsweetened baking chocolate
- 2 tablespoons canola oil
- ½ cup pumpkin puree (from 15-oz can; not pumpkin pie mix)
- ½ cup sugar
- 1 teaspoon vanilla
- 2 egg whites
- ½ cup fat-free plain Greek yogurt
- 3 tablespoons strong brewed coffee
- Strawberry halves, if desired
- 1¼ cups frozen (thawed) fat-free whipped topping (from 8-oz container)
- 2 teaspoons unsweetened baking cocoa

1 Heat oven to 350°F. Spray 9-inch round cake pan with cooking spray.

2 In small bowl, stir flour, baking powder and baking soda; set aside.

3 In medium microwavable bowl, microwave chocolate and oil uncovered on High 1 to 2 minutes, stirring once, until chocolate can be stirred smooth. Add pumpkin, sugar, vanilla and egg whites and beat with spoon or whisk until smooth.

4 In small bowl, mix yogurt and coffee. Beat flour mixture and yogurt mixture alternately into chocolate mixture, beating just until blended. Spoon into pan.

5 Bake 22 to 25 minutes or until set in center when touched. Cool 10 minutes; remove from pan to cooling rack. Serve warm or cool.

6 Just before serving, garnish with strawberry halves. Serve with whipped topping; sprinkle with cocoa.

1 SERVING Calories 180; Total Fat 6g (Saturated Fat 2.5g, Trans Fat 0g); Cholesterol 0mg; Sodium 160mg; Total Carbohydrate 25g (Dietary Fiber 2g); Protein 4g **CARBOHYDRATE CHOICES:** 1½

Betty's Kitchen Tip A simple way to get a nice, even sprinkle of cocoa powder is to put it into a small fine-mesh strainer. Hold it over the cake with one hand; with your other hand, tap the handle with a spoon.

Yogurt, whipped topping and chocolate cookies are all you need to make this lovely low-fat frozen dessert.

Frozen Chocolate Wafer–Raspberry Torte

PREP TIME: 10 Minutes / **START TO FINISH:** 4 Hours 10 Minutes / *14 servings*

4 containers (6 oz each) raspberry fat-free yogurt

1 cup frozen (thawed) fat-free whipped topping (from 8-oz container)

1 package (9 oz) thin chocolate wafer cookies

⅓ cup fresh raspberries

3 or 4 fresh mint leaves

1 Line 8×4-inch loaf pan with plastic wrap, leaving ends hanging over sides of pan.

2 In medium bowl, mix yogurt and whipped topping. Spoon yogurt mixture into pan about halfway up sides of pan. Arrange wafer cookies vertically across pan, making 4 rows of 9 or 10 cookies per row, filling length of pan. Spoon remaining yogurt mixture over cookies.

3 Cover top with plastic wrap. Freeze 4 to 8 hours. When ready to serve, dip bottom half of pan into hot water about 1 minute to loosen yogurt mixture. Use plastic wrap to lift torte from pan; place on serving plate. Garnish with raspberries and mint leaves. Cut into slices. Serve immediately.

1 SERVING Calories 140; Total Fat 3g (Saturated Fat 1g, Trans Fat 0g); Cholesterol 0mg; Sodium 160mg; Total Carbohydrate 25g (Dietary Fiber 1g); Protein 3g **CARBOHYDRATE CHOICES:** 1½

Betty's Kitchen Tip The dessert will be easier to cut If you let it stand in the refrigerator 15 minutes before slicing. Use a thin chef's knife for best results.

The light and airy texture of angel food cake has always made it a popular choice for an occasional treat. Adding mini chocolate chips, chocolate sauce and raspberries makes it special enough for celebrations yet easy enough for an anytime sweet.

CARB CHOICES 2½

Chocolate Chip Angel Food Cake

PREP TIME: 10 Minutes / **START TO FINISH:** 3 Hours / *16 servings*

1 box (1 lb) Betty Crocker™ white angel food cake mix

1¼ cups water

½ cup miniature semisweet chocolate chips

⅔ cup chocolate-flavor syrup

2 cups fresh raspberries

1 Move oven rack to lowest position; remove other racks. Heat oven to 350°F. Make cake mix as directed on box—except gently stir chocolate chips into batter. Bake, cool and remove from pan as directed.

2 To serve, drizzle each slice with 2 teaspoons chocolate syrup; garnish with berries.

1 SERVING Calories 180; Total Fat 2g (Saturated Fat 1g, Trans Fat 0g); Cholesterol 0mg; Sodium 250mg; Total Carbohydrate 38g (Dietary Fiber 1g); Protein 3g **CARBOHYDRATE CHOICES:** 2½

The creamy, sweet comfort of old-fashioned rice pudding is made easy in the slow cooker! Evaporated milk adds a richness and creaminess to the rice without curdling. Add an extra dash of cinnamon over servings, if you like.

CARB CHOICES 1½

Brown Rice Pudding

PREP TIME: 15 Minutes / **START TO FINISH:** 4 Hours / *12 servings (½ cup each)*

½ cup uncooked regular long-grain brown rice

1⅓ cups water

½ cup sugar

2 tablespoons butter, melted

1 teaspoon ground cinnamon

1 teaspoon vanilla

2 cans (12 oz each) evaporated milk

Additional ground cinnamon, if desired

1 Spray 3½-quart slow cooker with cooking spray.

2 In 1-quart saucepan, heat rice and water to boiling over medium heat; cover. Reduce heat to low; cook 45 to 50 minutes or until rice is tender and liquid is absorbed.

3 Add cooked rice to slow cooker; stir in remaining ingredients until well mixed.

4 Cover; cook on Low heat setting 2 hours. Remove cover and stir. Re-cover; cook 30 to 40 minutes longer or until most of liquid is absorbed. Turn off heat. Remove cover; stir. Let stand 15 minutes before serving. Serve warm sprinkled with additional cinnamon.

1 SERVING Calories 150; Total Fat 3.5g (Saturated Fat 2g, Trans Fat 0g); Cholesterol 5mg; Sodium 75mg; Total Carbohydrate 24g (Dietary Fiber 0g); Protein 4g **CARBOHYDRATE CHOICES:** 1½

Betty's Kitchen Tip Using cooked long-grain brown rice (without salt, oil or butter) in the slow cooker is essential to the success of this recipe. Do not use uncooked rice, instant rice, parboiled rice or precooked rice, as many of these contain oil to prevent sticking, which will affect the recipe. Uncooked or parboiled rice will be crunchy even after the long cooking; instant rice results in a mealy, grainy texture.

Betty's Kitchen Tip It's important to stir rice mixture after 2 hours of cook time to ensure even cooking, and to prevent burning.

Betty's Kitchen Tip For the most tender, evenly cooked results, make sure to cook rice pudding on low heat only. Rice pudding cooked on high heat will be crunchy and dry, and will burn onto the edges of the slow cooker.

This is such a simple dessert to put together—perfect for when strawberries are at the peak of their growing season.

CARB CHOICES 2

Strawberry-Lemon Shortcake Bowl

PREP TIME: 5 Minutes / **START TO FINISH:** 5 Minutes / *1 serving*

- ¼ cup light vanilla yogurt
- ¼ cup frozen (thawed) fat-free whipped topping
- ¾ cup fresh strawberries, hulled and cut in quarters
- ¼ cup gluten-free O-shaped honey-nut cereal
- ⅛ teaspoon lemon zest

1 In small bowl, place yogurt. Carefully stir in whipped topping until well mixed.

2 In serving bowl, place strawberries; top with yogurt mixture, cereal and lemon zest.

1 SERVING Calories 170; Total Fat 1.5g (Saturated Fat 1g, Trans Fat 0g); Cholesterol 0mg; Sodium 115mg; Total Carbohydrate 33g (Dietary Fiber 3g); Protein 4g **CARBOHYDRATE CHOICES:** 2

All the flavors and textures of a s'more in a manageable portion . . . and without the need for a campfire!

S'mores Candy Bark

PREP TIME: 20 Minutes / **START TO FINISH:** 1 Hour / *32 servings*

3 cups semisweet chocolate chips (about 18 oz)

¼ cup white vanilla baking chips

1 cup honey graham cereal squares

½ cup miniature marshmallows

1 Spray large cookie sheet with cooking spray; line with cooking parchment paper or waxed paper.

2 In large microwavable bowl, microwave chocolate chips uncovered on High 2 minutes, stirring after each minute. Continue microwaving and stirring in 15-second intervals until melted and smooth.

3 Pour melted chocolate onto cookie sheet. Use offset metal spatula to spread evenly into 10×13-inch rectangle, about ¼ inch thick.

4 In small microwavable bowl, microwave white vanilla baking chips uncovered on Medium (50%) 30 to 60 seconds. Continue microwaving in 15-second increments until chips can be stirred smooth. Drizzle over chocolate layer on cookie sheet.

5 Immediately sprinkle cereal and marshmallows over top; press into melted chocolate to help pieces stick. Refrigerate uncovered about 30 minutes or until firm. Break into pieces. Store covered in refrigerator.

1 SERVING Calories 80; Total Fat 4g (Saturated Fat 2.5g, Trans Fat 0g); Cholesterol 0mg; Sodium 10mg; Total Carbohydrate 10g (Dietary Fiber 0g); Protein 0g **CARBOHYDRATE CHOICES:** ½

Betty's Kitchen Tip Spraying the cookie sheet with cooking spray before placing the cooking parchment paper on top helps the paper stay in place while you spread the chocolate.

One recipe makes enough candies to keep some for yourself and to share. For a gift for practically any occasion, place each candy in a mini paper muffin cup and arrange the cups in a decorative tin or box.

CARB CHOICES

1/2

Buckeye Fudge

PREP TIME: 15 Minutes / **START TO FINISH:** 2 Hours 45 Minutes / *64 pieces*

3 cups peanut butter chips (about 18 oz)

1 can (14 oz) sweetened condensed milk (not evaporated)

½ cup creamy peanut butter

⅓ cup finely chopped cocktail peanuts

1 cup dark chocolate chips (about 6 oz)

½ cup whipping cream

1 Line 9-inch square pan with foil, leaving ends hanging over sides of pan. Spray foil with cooking spray.

2 In large microwavable bowl, microwave peanut butter chips uncovered on Medium (50%) 3 to 4 minutes, stirring well after each minute, until melted and smooth.

3 Stir in condensed milk, peanut butter and peanuts until blended. (Mixture will be thick.) Spread evenly in pan. Refrigerate 30 minutes.

4 In small microwavable bowl, microwave chocolate chips and cream uncovered on High 1 minute to 1 minute 30 seconds, stirring every 30 seconds, until smooth. Spread evenly over chilled fudge. Refrigerate about 2 hours or until topping is set.

5 Use foil to lift fudge from pan. Cut into 8 rows by 8 rows. Store in covered container in refrigerator up to 1 week.

1 PIECE Calories 107; Total Fat 6g (Saturated Fat 2g, Trans Fat 0g); Cholesterol 4mg; Sodium 47mg; Total Carbohydrate 12g (Dietary Fiber 1g); Protein 2g **CARBOHYDRATE CHOICES:** ½

Betty's Kitchen Tip Peanut butter chips can be very heat sensitive, so it is important to reduce the power level when melting them in the microwave.

Betty's Kitchen Tip To line pan with foil, turn pan upside down. Tear off a piece of foil longer than the pan. Smooth foil around pan bottom, then remove. Turn pan over, and gently fit shaped foil into pan. When fudge is cooled completely, lift out of pan by foil "handles," peel back foil and cut into pieces.

Using peach preserves enhances the peach flavor and adds a hint of sweetness without additional sugar.

Peach Ice Cream

PREP TIME: 20 Minutes / **START TO FINISH:** 4 Hours 40 Minutes / *8 servings (about ½ cup each)*

- 2 eggs
- 1 package (12 oz) frozen unsweetened sliced peaches, thawed
- ⅓ cup peach preserves
- 2 tablespoons water
- 1 envelope unflavored gelatin
- 2 cups 2% ultrafiltered lactose-free milk
- 1 teaspoon vanilla
- ¼ teaspoon almond extract

1 In small bowl, beat eggs with fork or whisk; set aside. In medium heatproof bowl, mash peaches with potato masher or break up until slightly chunky; set aside.

2 In 2-quart saucepan, stir preserves, water, and gelatin. Cook over medium heat 1 to 2 minutes, stirring frequently, or until preserves are melted and gelatin is dissolved. Stir in milk. Cook over medium heat, stirring constantly, until mixture almost starts to boil (do not allow to boil or it will curdle); remove from heat. Gradually stir at least ½ cup of hot milk mixture into eggs, then stir back into mixture in saucepan. Return to medium heat and cook about 1 minute, stirring constantly, or just until mixture thickens and coats back of spoon (do not boil); instant-read thermometer should read about 175°F. Remove from heat and stir in vanilla and almond extract.

3 Pour milk mixture into bowl with peaches; stir to mix. Cover with plastic wrap and refrigerate 3 to 4 hours, stirring occasionally, until chilled. Mixture will be thick. (At this point mixture can be stored in refrigerator up to 24 hours before completing recipe.)

4 Pour mixture into 1½- or 2-quart ice cream maker and freeze according to manufacturer's directions. Serve immediately. To freeze until hard, spoon ice cream into freezer-safe food storage container. Cover; freeze at least 6 hours or until hard. Let frozen ice cream stand at room temperature 30 minutes before serving.

1 SERVING Calories 100; Total Fat 2.5g (Saturated Fat 1g, Trans Fat 0g); Cholesterol 50mg; Sodium 50mg; Total Carbohydrate 15g (Dietary Fiber 0g); Protein 4g **CARBOHYDRATE CHOICES:** 1

Peach-Basil Ice Cream Add 2 tablespoons chopped fresh basil leaves with the milk in Step 3. Garnish with additional basil, if desired.

Peach-Basil
Ice Cream

This cold, refreshing treat would be a perfect pick-me-up on a hot day. Stirring the mixture every half hour will help give the granita a lovely icy, granular texture, without letting it become one big coffee ice cube! Once it's frozen, you can store it in a freezer container to enjoy any time. You may need to let the granita stand at room temperature a few minutes and loosen it with a fork before serving.

CARB CHOICES

1

Mocha Granita

PREP TIME: 5 Minutes / **START TO FINISH:** 2 Hours 35 Minutes / *7 servings (1 cup each)*

3 cups cold strong brewed coffee

1 cup vanilla or light chocolate soymilk

½ cup sugar

2 tablespoons unsweetened baking cocoa

Mint sprigs, if desired

1 Place 13×9-inch pan in freezer to chill. Meanwhile, in medium bowl, stir together all ingredients until sugar and cocoa is dissolved.

2 Pour mixture into chilled pan; freeze 30 minutes. When ice crystals begin to form at edges of pan, stir mixture with fork. Freeze about 2 hours longer, stirring every 30 minutes, until completely frozen.

3 To serve, scoop into individual dessert bowls and garnish with mint sprigs.

1 SERVING Calories 80; Total Fat 0.5g (Saturated Fat 0g, Trans Fat 0g); Cholesterol 0mg; Sodium 25mg; Total Carbohydrate 17g (Dietary Fiber 0g); Protein 1g **CARBOHYDRATE CHOICES:** 1

Make Ahead Scoop into stemmed dishes or glass bowls and freeze until dessert time.

This is what happens when shortcake meets s'mores meets cake pops . . . total deliciousness! If you like, sprinkle the platter with additional chocolate chips and vegan miniature marshmallows for the total s'mores theme. Just remember these are "extra" in terms of carbs and other nutrients.

CARB CHOICES

1

S'more Shortcake Pops

PREP TIME: 25 Minutes / **START TO FINISH:** 1 Hour 25 Minutes / *36 shortcake pops*

2⅓ cups Bisquick Heart Smart™ mix

2 containers (6-oz each) vanilla fat-free yogurt

2 tablespoons sugar

2 tablespoons butter, melted

1 jar (7 oz) marshmallow creme (1½ cups)

36 craft sticks (flat wooden sticks with round ends)

1 bag (11.5 oz) milk chocolate chips (2 cups)

1 teaspoon vegetable shortening

2 tablespoons graham cracker crumbs

1 block polystyrene foam

1 Heat oven to 425°F. In medium bowl, stir Bisquick mix, yogurt, sugar and butter until soft dough forms. Drop in 6 mounds from spoon onto ungreased cookie sheet.

2 Bake 10 to 12 minutes or until golden brown. Remove from cookie sheet to cooling rack. Cool completely, about 30 minutes.

3 Crumble shortcake into large bowl. Add marshmallow creme; mix with spoon until dough forms. Shape into 36 (1-inch) balls; mixture will be sticky. Place balls on cookie sheet. Insert 1 craft stick halfway into each shortcake ball; gently squeeze dough around stick. Freeze, uncovered, 15 minutes.

4 Meanwhile, in medium microwavable bowl, microwave chocolate chips and shortening uncovered on High 1 minute, stirring once, until melted and can be stirred smooth.

5 Remove shortcake balls from freezer a few at a time. One at a time, gently dip balls two-thirds of the way into chocolate mixture; tap off excess. Sprinkle with graham cracker crumbs. Poke opposite end of stick into foam block. Let stand until set. Store pops covered in refrigerator. To serve, let stand uncovered at room temperature 15 minutes.

1 SHORTCAKE POP Calories 100; Total Fat 4g (Saturated Fat 2g, Trans Fat 0g); Cholesterol 0mg; Sodium 60mg; Total Carbohydrate 14g (Dietary Fiber 0g); Protein 1g **CARBOHYDRATE CHOICES:** 1

Yogurt thaws quickly, so remove cups from freezer just a few minutes before serving.

CARB CHOICES

1

Frozen Mocha Mint Cups

PREP TIME: 15 Minutes / **START TO FINISH:** 1 Hour 15 Minutes / *9 cups*

½ cup chocolate cookie crumbs

1 tablespoon butter, melted

1 teaspoon hot water

1 teaspoon espresso or coffee granules

3 containers (6 oz each) light very vanilla yogurt

3 tablespoons chocolate-flavor syrup

⅛ teaspoon mint extract

⅔ cup frozen (thawed) whipped topping (from 8-oz container)

3 thin rectangular crème de menthe chocolate candies, unwrapped, chopped

1 Place foil or paper baking cup in each of 9 regular-size muffin cups. Mix cookie crumbs and butter; firmly press about 1 tablespoon mixture in bottom of each baking cup.

2 In medium bowl, mix water and espresso granules until dissolved. Stir in yogurt, chocolate syrup and mint extract until well mixed. Spoon and spread about 3 tablespoons of the yogurt mixture over crumbs in each cup. Gently spread about 1 tablespoon whipped topping on each.

3 Freeze until firm, at least 1 hour. Garnish with chopped candies.

1 CUP Calories 110; Total Fat 4g (Saturated Fat 2.5g, Trans Fat 0g); Cholesterol 0mg; Sodium 80mg; Total Carbohydrate 16g (Dietary Fiber 0g); Protein 2g **CARBOHYDRATE CHOICES:** 1

These thirst-quenching pops taste like you're having a cocktail—but using rum extract, rather than real rum. Adding a lime slice garnish really makes them feel like a frozen celebration!

CARB CHOICES

1

Watermelon Mojito Cocktail Pops

PREP TIME: 10 Minutes / **START TO FINISH:** 8 Hours 10 Minutes / *5 pops*

- 2 **cups chopped seedless watermelon or watermelon, seeded**
- 3 **tablespoons organic sugar**
- 3 **tablespoons fresh lime juice**
- 3 **tablespoons water**

- 1 **teaspoon rum extract**
- 4 **small fresh mint leaves**
- 5 **(5-oz) paper cups**
- 5 **craft sticks (flat wooden sticks with round ends)**
  Lime slices, if desired

1 In blender, place watermelon, sugar, lime juice, water, rum extract and mint. Cover; blend until smooth.

2 Divide mixture evenly among paper cups. Cover cups with foil; insert craft stick into center of each pop. Freeze about 8 hours or until frozen.

3 Store in freezer up to 2 months. To serve, remove foil; peel off paper cups. Garnish pops with lime slices.

1 POP Calories 60; Total Fat 0g (Saturated Fat 0g, Trans Fat 0g); Cholesterol 0mg; Sodium 0mg; Total Carbohydrate 13g (Dietary Fiber 0g); Protein 0g **CARBOHYDRATE CHOICES:** 1

Keep a stash of the remaining sandwich treats in the freezer for a yummy occasional treat for you, your family or for when guests drop by.

CARB CHOICES

1

Mini Frozen Chocolate Sandwiches

PREP TIME: 20 Minutes / **START TO FINISH:** 1 Hour 20 Minutes / *20 sandwiches*

1 container (6 oz) strawberry fat-free yogurt

½ cup frozen (thawed) fat-free or reduced-fat whipped topping (from a 8-oz container)

40 thin chocolate wafer cookies (from 9-oz package)

1 In small bowl, gently fold yogurt and whipped topping until blended. Place 20 cookies bottom side up onto baking sheet. Spoon 1 scant tablespoon yogurt mixture onto each cookie. Top with remaining cookies, bottom down.

2 Cover with foil. Freeze at least 1 hour or until centers are frozen. Transfer to resealable freezer plastic bag. Store in freezer up to 1 month.

1 SANDWICH Calories 70; Total Fat 2g (Saturated Fat 0.5g, Trans Fat 0g); Cholesterol 0mg; Sodium 95mg; Total Carbohydrate 11g (Dietary Fiber 0g); Protein 1g **CARBOHYDRATE CHOICES:** 1

To remove pops from molds, run sides of molds under cool water for a few seconds; pops will slide out easily.

Cold Brew Yogurt Pops

PREP TIME: 10 Minutes / **START TO FINISH:** 2 Hours 10 Minutes / *6 pops*

¾ cup vanilla Greek yogurt

2 tablespoons chopped special dark chocolate candy bar (from 3.1-oz bar)

1 (11-oz) bottle sweetened or unsweetened cold brew coffee

1 In small bowl, mix yogurt and chocolate. Pour 2 tablespoons coffee into each of 6 (3-oz) ice pop molds; carefully spoon 2 tablespoons yogurt mixture on top of the coffee. Repeat with remaining coffee. Cover with mold tops.

2 Freeze pops at least 2 hours or until frozen. To serve, remove pops from molds.

1 POP Calories 45; Total Fat 1.5g (Saturated Fat 1g, Trans Fat 0g); Cholesterol 0mg; Sodium 15mg; Total Carbohydrate 5g (Dietary Fiber 0g); Protein 2g **CARBOHYDRATE CHOICES:** ½

Betty's Kitchen Tip If you don't have ice pop molds you can use 6 (3-oz) paper cups instead. Cover cups with foil and insert craft stick into center of each pop. Freeze as directed. To serve, peel off paper cups.

Sometimes berry yogurt can look more gray than berry colored. A half teaspoon of beet juice or a drop of liquid red food color can help when making these pies.

CARB CHOICES
1/2

Frozen Yogurt Mini Pies

PREP TIME: 15 Minutes / **START TO FINISH:** 1 Hour 20 Minutes / *15 mini pies*

¾ cup graham cracker crumbs (from about 6 rectangles)

2 tablespoons butter, melted

2 containers (6 oz each) original mixed berry yogurt

15 fresh blueberries or raspberries

1 Place paper baking cup in each of 15 mini muffin cups.

2 In small bowl, stir graham cracker crumbs and butter until mixed. Spoon and press 1 tablespoon mixture into bottom of each muffin cup. Top each with 1 rounded tablespoon yogurt and 1 berry.

3 Freeze about 1 hour or until frozen. Let stand 5 minutes at room temperature before serving.

1 MINI PIE Calories 50; Total Fat 2g (Saturated Fat 1g, Trans Fat 0g); Cholesterol 5mg; Sodium 45mg; Total Carbohydrate 7g (Dietary Fiber 0g); Protein 1g **CARBOHYDRATE CHOICES:** ½

Betty's Kitchen Tip Keep these bite-size frozen berry pies on hand for a perfect cold summertime snack or dessert.

Betty's Kitchen Tip The frozen pies can be stored in a freezer-safe food storage container in the freezer up to 1 month. Loosely cover the pies with plastic wrap; cover with lid. Let stand as directed in Step 3 before serving.

If you don't have ice pop molds, small paper cups make a nice substitute. Serve the pops in the cups at gatherings, to catch any drips that might happen before they are eaten.

Strawberry Mango Lime Pops

PREP TIME: 15 Minutes / **START TO FINISH:** 6 Hours 15 Minutes / *4 pops*

2 teaspoons honey

1 container (6 oz) light Key lime pie yogurt

4 (4 oz) ice pop molds or 4 (5-oz) disposable paper cups

½ cup chopped fresh strawberries

1 container (6 oz) original strawberry mango yogurt

4 craft sticks (flat wooden sticks with round ends)

1 Stir 1 teaspoon of the honey into lime yogurt until blended. Spoon evenly among ice pop molds or disposable paper cups.

2 Divide strawberries evenly among molds. Stir remaining teaspoon honey into strawberry-mango yogurt until blended; spoon evenly among molds. Cover with mold tops; if using cups, cover with foil; insert craft stick into center of each pop.

3 Freeze about 6 hours or until completely frozen. To serve, remove pops from molds. (If pops don't release from molds, run them under warm water for a few seconds; pull out from molds.) If using cups, peel cups from pops.

1 POP Calories 100; Total Fat 1g (Saturated Fat 1g, Trans Fat 0g); Cholesterol 5mg; Sodium 50mg; Total Carbohydrate 18g (Dietary Fiber 0g); Protein 3g **CARBOHYDRATE CHOICES:** 1

The stripes of these delicious frozen treats are fun but take time to achieve. If you like, you can make the pops half strawberry and half green smoothie: Divide all of the strawberry mixture among the paper cups or ice pop molds; freeze until frozen; repeat with the green smoothie layer, and you can get to the eating part more quickly!

CARB CHOICES

1

Strawberry–Green Smoothie Pops

PREP TIME: 15 Minutes / **START TO FINISH:** 8 Hours 15 Minutes / *5 pops*

1 container (5.3 oz) vegetarian-friendly strawberry Greek yogurt alternative

1 cup sliced fresh strawberries

A few drops red food color, if desired

5 (5-oz) paper cups and 5 craft sticks (flat wooden sticks with round ends) or 5 (4-oz) ice pop molds

1 container (6 oz) original Key lime pie yogurt or 1 container (5.3 oz) Greek coconut yogurt

1 cup packed fresh baby spinach leaves

¼ cup apple juice

1 In blender, place yogurt, strawberries and food color. Cover; blend until smooth. Spoon 2 tablespoons mixture into each cup. Cover cups with foil; insert craft stick into center of each pop. (Or fill ice pop molds as for cups.) Put remaining mixture in bowl; cover and refrigerate. Freeze pops about 2 hours or until frozen.

2 In blender, place Key lime pie yogurt, spinach and apple juice. Cover; blend until smooth. When first layer is frozen, remove foil from pops. Pour about 1½ tablespoons spinach mixture in each cup over frozen layer. Put remaining mixture in bowl; cover and refrigerate. Return foil to pops to support sticks. Freeze about 2 hours or until frozen.

3 Repeat layers with remaining strawberry and spinach mixtures, freezing at least 2 hours between layers. To serve, peel paper from pops.

1 POP Calories 80; Total Fat 1.5g (Saturated Fat 1g, Trans Fat 0g); Cholesterol 5mg; Sodium 40mg; Total Carbohydrate 12g (Dietary Fiber 1g); Protein 4g **CARBOHYDRATE CHOICES:** 1

Betty's Kitchen Tip For a great layered look, freezing completely between layers is necessary so colors do not mix with each other.

Like your drinks extra bubbly? Try substituting chilled diet tonic water for the sparkling water.

CARB CHOICES

1/2

Watermelon-Strawberry Agua Fresca

PREP TIME: 25 Minutes / **START TO FINISH:** 25 Minutes / *6 servings (about ¾ cup each)*

3 cups cubed seedless watermelon

2 cups halved fresh strawberries

2 tablespoons fresh lime juice

¼ cup packed fresh mint or cilantro leaves

3 cups chilled sparkling water

1 In blender or food processor, place watermelon, strawberries, and lime juice. Cover and blend about 30 seconds or until smooth. Place large fine-mesh strainer over medium bowl. Pour fruit mixture into strainer; let stand 15 minutes, stirring occasionally. Discard fruit pulp in strainer.

2 In large pitcher, place mint leaves; press with the back of spoon to bruise leaves. Add strained fruit mixture to pitcher. Add sparkling water; stir gently to mix. Serve over ice.

1 SERVING Calories 45; Total Fat 0g (Saturated Fat 0g, Trans Fat 0g); Cholesterol 0mg; Sodium 0mg; Total Carbohydrate 10g (Dietary Fiber 1g); Protein 1g **CARBOHYDRATE CHOICES:** ½

Betty's Kitchen Tip If you like, garnish this beautiful drink with thin sticks of watermelon and mint leaves.

Sometimes people think they are hungry when they are thirsty instead. Smoothies like this one will solve either issue in a most delicious way!

Strawberry Smoothies

PREP TIME: 5 Minutes / **START TO FINISH:** 5 Minutes / *2 servings (1 cup each)*

1 container (6 oz) vegetarian-friendly strawberry low-fat yogurt alternative

1 cup fresh strawberry halves or frozen unsweetened whole strawberries

¾ cup fat-free (skim) milk

2 tablespoons original bran cereal shreds

Additional strawberries cut in half, if desired

1 In blender, place all ingredients. Cover; blend on high speed 10 seconds. Scrape down sides of blender. Cover; blend about 20 seconds longer or until smooth.

2 Pour into 2 glasses. Garnish with additional strawberry halves. Serve immediately.

1 SERVING Calories 160; Total Fat 1.5g (Saturated Fat 0.5g, Trans Fat 0g); Cholesterol 5mg; Sodium 100mg; Total Carbohydrate 30g (Dietary Fiber 3g); Protein 7g **CARBOHYDRATE CHOICES:** 2

Betty's Kitchen Tip For a smoother consistency, crush cereal in a small resealable food-storage plastic bag with a rolling pin before adding it to ingredients in blender.

FAST / GLUTEN FREE / VEGETARIAN

Here's a great way to enjoy a root beer float on a healthy eating plan. But it's a dilemma . . . do you drink the root beer right away, before the yogurt cubes melt, or let the yogurt cubes melt before you enjoy the float? You may want to make this recipe again and again to decide which way to enjoy it.

CARB CHOICES
½

Skinny Root Beer Floats

PREP TIME: 5 Minutes / **START TO FINISH:** 2 Hours / *2 servings*

- **1 container (5.3 oz) Greek 100 protein vanilla yogurt**
- **2 cans (12 oz each) chilled diet root beer**

1 Place 1 generous tablespoon yogurt into each of 8 sections of ice cube tray. Freeze about 2 hours or until firm.

2 In each of 2 tall drinking glasses, place 4 yogurt cubes. Pour root beer over cubes. Serve immediately.

1 SERVING Calories 50; Total Fat 0g (Saturated Fat 0g, Trans Fat 0g); Cholesterol 0mg; Sodium 90mg; Total Carbohydrate 5g (Dietary Fiber 0g); Protein 7g **CARBOHYDRATE CHOICES:** ½

Thirst-quenching and delicious, these two-ingredient floats can be a nice treat—once in a while. Try using other small freezer molds to freeze the yogurt for a fun way to add joy to a beverage!

CARB CHOICES

1/2

Skinny Orange Cream Floats

PREP TIME: 5 Minutes / START TO FINISH: 2 Hours / *2 servings*

1 container (5.3 oz) Greek 100 protein vanilla yogurt

2 cans (12 oz each) chilled diet orange carbonated beverage

1 Place 1 generous tablespoon yogurt into each of 8 sections of ice cube tray. Freeze about 2 hours or until firm.

2 In each of two tall drinking glasses, place 4 yogurt cubes. Pour beverage over cubes. Serve immediately.

1 SERVING Calories 50; Total Fat 0g (Saturated Fat 0g, Trans Fat 0g); Cholesterol 0mg; Sodium 50mg; Total Carbohydrate 5g (Dietary Fiber 0g); Protein 8g **CARBOHYDRATE CHOICES:** ½

Zero-proof liqueur alternatives are popping up in more liquor stores all the time. Look for them in larger stores and online. If you keep frozen yogurt cubes and Key lime juice on hand, you'll be able to mix these up at a moment's notice.

CARB CHOICES

1

Spirit-Free Key Lime Gin and Tonic

PREP TIME: 5 Minutes / START TO FINISH: 2 Hours / *1 serving*

1 container (5.3 oz) Greek 100 protein vanilla yogurt

2 oz (¼ cup) spirit-free gin

6 oz (¾ cup) diet tonic water

1 to 3 teaspoons fresh or bottled Key lime juice

1 Key lime slice

1 Place 1 generous tablespoon yogurt into each of 3 sections of ice cube tray. Freeze about 2 hours or until firm. (Use remaining yogurt to make additional cubes, or cover and refrigerate for another use.)

2 In highball glass, place 3 yogurt cubes. Add gin, tonic water and 1 teaspoon lime juice (or more to taste); stir. Garnish with lime slice and serve immediately.

1 SERVING Calories 110; Total Fat 0g (Saturated Fat 0g, Trans Fat 0g); Cholesterol 0mg; Sodium 95mg; Total Carbohydrate 11g (Dietary Fiber 0g); Protein 15g **CARBOHYDRATE CHOICES:** 1

From left to right: Spirit-Free Key Lime Gin and
Tonic (left), Skinny Root Bear Floats (page 339),
Skinny Orange Cream Floats (left)

For a fun garnish, place the lime wedges and some mango chunks or thin slices decorative picks in each glass.

CARB CHOICES

2

Zero Proof Frozen Mango Margaritas

PREP TIME: 10 Minutes / **START TO FINISH:** 10 Minutes / *4 servings*

5 lime wedges (from one lime)

4 tablespoons organic sugar

1 teaspoon ground red pepper (cayenne)

2 cups diced fresh mango

2 cups cracked ice

⅓ cup vegan alcohol-free tequila alternative

2 tablespoons fresh orange juice

2 tablespoons fresh lime juice

Additional mango chunks or slices, if desired

1 Rub 1 of the lime wedges around rim of 4 margarita glasses. Mix 2 tablespoons of the sugar and the red pepper on small flat plate; dip rim of each glass into sugar.

2 In blender, place remaining 2 tablespoons sugar, the mango, ice, tequila alternative and orange and lime juices. Cover; blend on high speed 1 to 2 minutes or until smooth and slushy. Pour into glasses. Serve with remaining lime wedges and mango.

1 SERVING Calories 120; Total Fat 0g (Saturated Fat 0g, Trans Fat 0g); Cholesterol 0mg; Sodium 10mg; Total Carbohydrate 27g (Dietary Fiber 1g); Protein 0g **CARBOHYDRATE CHOICES:** 2

Betty's Kitchen Tip Can't take the heat? Dip only half of the rim of your glass in the sugar mixture.

Betty's Kitchen Tip For smoothest results, use your blender's ice crush mode for the first few seconds to break up any big chunks of ice.

To mimic the dry, robust flavor of red wine, we had the genius idea to swap in black tea. Then we steeped a variety of spices in simple syrup for a burst of spiciness. Save the cinnamon stick and use it for a festive garnish with additional slices of oranges and limes.

CARB CHOICES 2

Spirit-Free Spiced Sangria Punch

PREP TIME: 20 Minutes / **START TO FINISH:** 3 Hours 40 Minutes / *9 servings (about 1 cup each)*

1 cup water

½ cup organic sugar

6 cinnamon sticks

2 teaspoons whole allspice

1½ teaspoons whole cloves

6 (¼-inch) slices gingerroot

3 black tea bags

2 cups organic pomegranate juice

1 cup organic white grape juice

1 cup organic orange juice

1 medium orange, thinly sliced

1 medium lime, thinly sliced

2 cans (12 oz each) chilled lime-flavored sparkling water

Ice cubes, if desired

1 In 1-quart saucepan, heat water, sugar, 4 of the cinnamon sticks, the allspice, cloves and gingerroot to boiling over medium-high heat. Reduce heat to low; simmer 15 minutes. Remove from heat. Add tea bags; steep 5 minutes. Remove tea bags; cool 1 hour. Strain into large pitcher; discard solids.

2 Add remaining 2 cinnamon sticks, pomegranate, white grape and orange juice, and orange and lime slices. Refrigerate at least 2 hours or until chilled.

3 Just before serving, stir in sparkling water. Serve over ice.

1 SERVING Calories 120; Total Fat 0g (Saturated Fat 0g, Trans Fat 0g); Cholesterol 0mg; Sodium 25mg; Total Carbohydrate 29g (Dietary Fiber 1g); Protein 0g **CARBOHYDRATE CHOICES:** 2

Betty's Kitchen Tip An orange slice cut in half and a slice of lime make a lovely garnish for each glass.

Metric Conversion Guide

VOLUME

U.S. UNITS	CANADIAN METRIC	AUSTRALIAN METRIC
¼ teaspoon	1 mL	1 ml
½ teaspoon	2 mL	2 ml
1 teaspoon	5 mL	5 ml
1 tablespoon	15 mL	20 ml
¼ cup	50 mL	60 ml
⅓ cup	75 mL	80 ml
½ cup	125 mL	125 ml
⅔ cup	150 mL	170 ml
¾ cup	175 mL	190 ml
1 cup	250 mL	250 ml
1 quart	1 liter	1 liter
1½ quarts	1.5 liters	1.5 liters
2 quarts	2 liters	2 liters
2½ quarts	2.5 liters	2.5 liters
3 quarts	3 liters	3 liters
4 quarts	4 liters	4 liters

WEIGHT

U.S. UNITS	CANADIAN METRIC	AUSTRALIAN METRIC
1 ounce	30 grams	30 grams
2 ounces	55 grams	60 grams
3 ounces	85 grams	90 grams
4 ounces (¼ pound)	115 grams	125 grams
8 ounces (½ pound)	225 grams	225 grams
16 ounces (1 pound)	455 grams	500 grams
1 pound	455 grams	0.5 kilogram

NOTE: The recipes in this cookbook have not been developed or tested using metric measures. When converting recipes to metric, some variations in quality may be noted.

MEASUREMENTS

INCHES	CENTIMETERS
1	2.5
2	5.0
3	7.5
4	10.0
5	12.5
6	15.0
7	17.5
8	20.5
9	23.0
10	25.5
11	28.0
12	30.5
13	33.0

TEMPERATURES

FAHRENHEIT	CELSIUS
32°	0°
212°	100°
250°	120°
275°	140°
300°	150°
325°	160°
350°	180°
375°	190°
400°	200°
425°	220°
450°	230°
475°	240°
500°	260°

Index

Note: Page references in *italics* indicate photographs.

Bibliography

1. "Healthy Living," American
    Diabetes Association,
    https://www.diabetes.org
    /healthy-living.

2. "Diabetes," Mayo Clinic,
    https://www.mayoclinic
    .org/diseases-conditions
    /diabetes/symptoms
    -causes/syc-20371444.

3. "Treatment Guide: Managing
    Diabetes," Cleveland Clinic,
    https://my.clevelandclinic
    .org/-/scassets/files/org
    /endocrinology-metabolism
    /managing-diabetes
    -treatment-guide.ashx?la
    =en.

4. "Diabetes Meal Planning,"
    Center for Disease Control
    and Prevention, https://
    www.cdc.gov/diabetes
    /managing/eat-well/meal
    -plan-method.html.